PHP Reference: Beginner to Intermediate PHP5

Mario Lurig

PHP Reference:

Beginner to Intermediate PHP5

ISBN: 978-1-4357-1590-5

FIRST EDITION

http://www.phpreferencebook.com

Cover art credit (PHP REFERENCE:), included with permission:

Leo Reynolds (www.flickr.com/lwr/) - 7 images

Patrick Goor (www.labworks.eu) - 3 images

Eva the Weaver (www.flickr.com/evaekeblad/) - 2 images

Duncan Cumming (www.flickr.com/duncan/) - 1 image

Contents

Preface

I taught myself PHP and MySQL and found myself, at times, without internet access and thus without search access to the PHP.net manual (http://www.php.net/manual/en/). Since coding was not my primary job, I needed a refresher on syntax, usage, and most of all, a reminder of how to code PHP without spending an hour debugging a silly mistake. I printed out reference sheets, cards, cheat sheets and tried to work off of them exclusively. However, I still found myself needing more than would fit on one page of 8.5" x 11" paper front and back. So, off I went to the web and the local bookstore. After spending some time with a few books, giving them a trial run, I ran into two major problems:

1. I spent most of the time weeding through extensive tutorials to find the keyword and answer I was looking for, sometimes fruitlessly.
2. Information was biased or surrounded by irrelevant and often confusing code that did little to explain the *what* of the function.

I figured I couldn't be the only one with this problem, and quickly found out that I wasn't alone thanks to a chance run-in at a local bookstore. Casual PHP programmers, sometimes away from the internet, wanting a quick reference book that assumes they have some experience with PHP and understood the basics while still needing a little clarification sometimes on the details. Therefore, this book was born.

For this edition, I decided to eliminate some of the more advanced aspects of PHP programming: object oriented programming, image manipulation/creation, secondary modules, and a few others. Secondarily, items such as mail handling, file manipulation, regular expressions, MySQL, sessions, and cookies were balanced for complexity and usability, usually excluding the more advanced uses, such as streams . Finally, this book is not an exhaustive collection of every PHP function, but a majority selection of those appropriate for beginner to intermediate programmers. The most common or effective functions are included and some aliases are left out to reduce confusion, such as including **is_int()** and not **is_long()**.

A few bits of nomenclature should be addressed and provided, to better understand the word/code used inside this book. In other words, here are some assumptions made inside this book that you should understand:

expr – An expression (*e.g.* $x == 1), including **boolean**
$variable – A **string**, **integer**, **float**, **array** or **boolean**[1]
$scalar - A **string**, **integer**, **float**, or **boolean**
$string – A **string** variable or its equivalent (*e.g.* "string" or 'string')
$array – An **array** variable or its equivalent (*e.g.* array('one' , 'two' , 'three'))
key – Represents the key (**integer** or **string**) of an **array** (*e.g.* $array[*key*])
value – In relation to an **array**, represents the **$variable** value (*e.g.* array('*value* '))

This book also shows all code using procedural PHP and standard syntax. However, you will find many tips will include the alternative syntax for control structures as to better allow you, the reader, to choose whichever you would prefer. Here is an example of both:

```
// Standard syntax
if ($x == 1) {
    echo 'Hello World!';
  } else {
    echo 'Goodbye World!';
}

// Alternative syntax
if ($x == 1):
    echo 'Hello World!';
  else:
    echo 'Goodbye World!';
endif;
```

Furthermore, the use of whitespace and indenting is for clarity and is completely up to your preference. Styles vary greatly in the community, so please be aware that the use of spaces or whitespace does not directly affect the PHP code.

The majority of the book is a collection of functions, their descriptions, example code, maybe an extra tip, and some related functions that may be of interest. All sample code will be accompanied by the sample output, and the output will have a gray background. The *definition* and *example* section is separated from the extraneous *tip* section by the use of three black clovers, centered on the line. It is meant as a simple visual clue to keep one from getting distracted or lost and confusing the next bit of information as required reading. All functions will be presented using the following formatting:

1 Boolean is usually used within an expression. While it is also evaluated as a variable, output results may vary and are noted within specific functions whenever possible

function name(input, [optional input])

Description/definition

Example:

```
Code with // comments
```

```
Output of code as seen through a web browser's output
```

See Also:

function – simplified and relevant definition
function – simplified and relevant definition

♣ ♣ ♣

{Optional Section} Tip to help with usage or trick on using it

```
Extra code
related to the tip
```

```
Output
{
    [0] => Of
    [1] => Code
}
```

Thanks, and enjoy the show!

Miscellaneous Things You Should Know

Not everything fits into a neat little category, nor does everything in PHP belong in this reference book. However, sometimes they deserve a quick note and a little attention and shall be included here.

PHP Code

For portability and compatibility, always use the long form.

Long form:
```
<?php expr ?>
```

Short form:
```
<? expr ?>
```

Short form equivalent of <? **echo** *expr* ?>
Note: *No closing semicolon (;) is required.*
```
<?= expr ?>
```

Semicolon (;)

All statements must end in a semicolon (;)! Otherwise, errors will be generated. If the error doesn't make sense, you probably are missing a semicolon somewhere!

Quotations

' ' (single quotes) – Content inside single quotes is evaluated literally. Therefore, $string actually means: (dollar sign)string, and does not represent the variable's value.

Example:

```
$string = 'Single Quotes';
echo '$string';
```

```
$string
```

" " (double quotes) – Variables inside double quotes are evaluated for their values.

Example:

```
$string = 'Double Quotes';
echo "$string";
```

```
Double Quotes
```

Backslash (Escape Character)

Escapes characters that should be evaluated literally when inside double quotations.

Example:

```
$string = 'Double Quotes';
echo "\$string is set as $string";
```

```
$string is set as Double Quotes
```

Special Characters

backslash (\ )
question mark (?)
single (') quotes
double (") quotes
dollar sign ($)

Example:

```
$string = 'Hello World!';
echo "The variable \$string contains \' $string \' \" \\";
```

```
The variable $string contains \' Hello World! \' " \
```

```
echo 'The variable \$string contains \' $string \' \" \\';
```

```
The variable \$string contains ' $string ' \" \
```

Comments

Single line, for everything to the right of the double *forward* slashes:

```
// This is a comment
```

Multiple lines, opening and closing tags:

/* */

```
/* This is
a comment */
```

Formatting Characters

`\n` – New line
`\r` – Carriage return
`\t` – Tab
`\b` – Backspace

define(*name, value* [, $boolean])

name – **$string**
value – **$scalar**
$boolean – [optional] *default*: FALSE, case-sensitive

Define a constant, a set value that is assigned globally, making it available to functions and classes without passing them directly as an argument.

Examples:

```
define('HELLO', 'Hello World!');
echo HELLO;
```

```
Hello World!
```

```
define('GREETINGS', 'Hello World!', TRUE);
echo GREETINGS;
echo greetings;
```

```
Hello World!Hello World!
```

Functions

```
function functionname([arguments]) { }
```

Functions can be placed anywhere in a page and will be available even if called above the actual function being created. The exception to this rule is if the function is only defined as part of a conditional statement, and is not available to be called until that conditional statement has been evaluated.

Examples:

```
hello();
 // Above the conditional statement, this will cause an error
if (0==0){
    function hello(){
      echo 'Hello!';
    }
}
```

```
Fatal error: Call to undefined function hello()
```

```
if (0==0){
    function hello(){
      echo 'Hello ';
    }
}
hello();
there();
function there(){
  echo 'there';
}
```

```
Hello there
```

Functions can have no arguments (as above), arguments passed to them, or default arguments with passed arguments as optional. The argument names are used within that function as variable names.

```
function args($a, $b){
  // Has no default values, requires two inputs
  echo "a = $a, b = $b";
}
args(1,2);
```

```
a = 1, b = 2
```

Some examples using the following function:

```
function args($a = 1, $b = 2){
  // Has default values set
  $c = $a + $b;
  echo "a = $a, b = $b, a+b = $c";
}
args();
```

```
a = 1, b = 2, a+b = 3
```

```
args(5,5);
```

```
a = 5, b = 5, a+b = 10
```

```
args(10);
```

```
a = 10, b = 2, a+b = 12
```

```
args($DoesNotExist,20); // Do not do this, send (NULL,20) instead
```

```
a = , b = 20, a+b = 20
```

Functions can also **return** a **$variable** (including an array):

```
function Add($one,$two){
    $total = $one + $two;
    return $total;
}
$a = 2;
$b = 3;
$result = Add($a,$b); // Assigns the value of $total to $result
echo $result;
```

```
5
```

♣ ♣ ♣

If multiple pages will refer to the same functions, create a separate **functions.php** file (name it whatever you like) and **require()** or **require_once()** with pages that will need to use those functions. For speed and file size, page specific functions should be included directly on the necessary page.

exit([$string])
die([$string])

Stops the current script and outputs the optional **$string**.

Example:

```
$result = @mysql_connect('db', 'user', 'pw')
        or die('Unable to connect to database!');
echo 'If it fails, this will never be seen';
```

```
Unable to connect to database!
```

***Note**: The above output would only display if it failed. If the @ was not present before mysql_connect(), PHP would output a warning as well.*

eval($string)

Evaluates a string as if it was code. This can be used to store code in a database and have it processed dynamically by PHP as if it were part of the page. All appropriate aspects of code must be included, such as escaping items with a backslash (\) and including a semicolon (;) at the end of the string.

Example:

```
$name = 'Mario';
$string = 'My name is $name.'; // Note the single quotes
echo $string;
$code = "\$evalstring = \" $string \" ;";
// Effect of backslash escape: $code = "$evalstring = " $string " ;";
eval($code); // eval($evalstring = " My name is $name " ;);
// $evalstring is the same as $string, except with double quotes now
echo $evalstring;
```

```
My name is $name. My name is Mario.
```

sleep($integer)

Pauses PHP for **$integer** amount of seconds before continuing.

Example:

```
sleep(2); // pause for 2 seconds
```

usleep($integer)

Pauses PHP for **$integer** amount of microseconds before continuing.

Example:

```
usleep(1000000); // pause for 1 second
```

uniqid([$scalar [, *entropy*]])

entropy – [optional] **$boolean** *default:* FALSE, 13 character output

Generate a unique ID based on the **$scalar**. If no input is given, the current time in microseconds is used automatically. This is best used in combination with other functions to generate a more unique value. If the **$scalar** is an empty string ('') and *entropy* is set to TRUE, a 26 character output is provided instead of a 13 character output.

Examples:

```
$id = uniqid();
echo $id;
```

```
47cc82c917c99
```

```
$random_id = uniqid(mt_rand());
echo $random_id;
```

```
63957259147cc82c917cdb
```

```
$md5 = md5($random_id);
echo $md5;
```

```
ea573adcdf20215bb391b82c2df3851f
```

See Also:

md5() – MD5 algorithm based encryption

setcookie(*name* [, *value*] [, *time*] [, *path*] [, *domain*] [, *secure*] [, *httponly*])

name – **$string**
value – [optional] **$string**
time – [optional] **$integer** *default*: till the end of the session
path – [optional] **$string** *default*: current directory
domain – [optional] **$string** *default*: current domain (*e.g.* http://www.example.com)
secure – [optional] **$boolean** *default*: FALSE, does not require a secure connection
httponly – [optional] **$boolean** *default*: FALSE, available to scripting languages

Sets a cookie[2], visible to the server on the next page load. To send then default value, use a set of single quotes ('') for each argument you want to skip except the *time* argument, which should use **0** to send the *default* value. In most cases, providing the *name, value, time,* and *domain* will cover most uses (with '' for *path*).

Examples:

```
setcookie('Cookie','Set till end of this session',0);
// This will display properly after the page has been reloaded
print_r($_COOKIE);
```

```
Array ( [Cookie] => Set till end of this session )
```

```
setcookie('Cookie','Set for 60 seconds for all subdomains of
example.com, such as www., mail., etc.',time()+60,'','.example.com');
print_r($_COOKIE);
```

```
Array ( [Cookie] => Set for 60 seconds for all subdomains of
example.com, such as www., mail., etc. )
```

Some common times used for expiration:
time()+60*60*24 is equal to 1 day
time()+60*60*24*30 is equal to 30 days
time()-1 is one second in the past, used to **expire/delete** a cookie

```
setcookie('Cookie','',time()-1);
// expires the Cookie named 'Cookie'. Note the empty string for value
```

urlencode($string)

Changes the formatting of **$string** to the proper format for passing through a URL, such as part of a GET query, returning the new string.

Example:

```
$string = 'Hello There! How are you?';
echo urlencode($string);
```

```
Hello+There%21+How+are+you%3F
```

urldecode($string)

Changes the formatting of **$string** from the URL compatible (such as a GET query) format to human readable format, returning the new string.

Example:

```
$string = 'Hello+There%21+How+are+you%3F';
echo urldecode($string);
```

```
Hello There! How are you?
```

2 Must be sent prior to any headers or anything else is sent to the page (including the <html> tag). See ob_start() for an easy way to make this work

get_magic_quotes_gpc()

Returns **0** if it is off, **1** otherwise.

Used to determine if magic quotes is on. This check is used for code portability and determining if the addition of backslashes is necessary for security purposes and preventing SQL injection. Magic_quotes_gpc processes GET/POST/Cookie data and, if turned on, automatically processes the above data every time with **addslashes()**.

Example:

```
if (get_magic_quotes_gpc()){
    echo 'Magic Quotes is on!';
  }else{
    echo 'Magic Quotes is NOT on, use addslashes()!';
}
```

```
// This is the default setting for PHP5 installations
Magic Quotes is NOT on, use addslashes()!
```

See Also:

addslashes() – Add backslashes to certain special characters in a string
stripslashes() – Remove backslashes from certain special characters in a string

phpinfo([*option*])

option – [optional] Used with a specific **$integer** or **$string** to display only a portion of **phpinfo()**. *Specific options excluded for simplicity.*

By default, **phpinfo()** will display everything about the PHP installation, including the modules, version, variables, etc.

Example:

```
phpinfo();
```

Display All PHP Errors and Warnings

To catch programming errors, mistakes, or make sure that PHP is not making any assumptions about your code, troubleshooting is best done with all PHP errors being displayed. The following two lines of code will enable this mode:

```
error_reporting(E_ALL);
ini_set('display_errors', '1');
```

mail(to, subject, message [*, headers*] [*, parameters*])

to – **$string**
subject – **$string**
message – **$string**
headers – [optional] **$string**
parameters – [optional] **$string**

This uses the sendmail binary which may not be configured or available depending on your system/setup. *This is included here for basic reference. The configuration and security concerns are outside of the scope of this book.*
Security consideration:
http://www.securephpwiki.com/index.php/Email_Injection

Example:

```
$to = 'johndoe@example.com';
$subject = 'Hello';
$message = 'Hi John Doe';
$headers = 'From: janedoe@example.com' . "\r\n" .
           'Reply-To: janedoe@example.com' . "\r\n" .
           'X-Mailer: PHP/' . phpversion();
mail($to, $subject, $message, $headers);
```

exec(*command* [*, output*] [*, return*])

command – **$string** to execute the external program
output – [optional] Variable name to assign all the output of the *command* as an array
return – [optional] Variable name to assign the return status as an **$integer**. Works only when *output* is also present.

The function will return the last line of the executed program's output. If the program fails to run and both *output* and *return* are both present, *return* will be most commonly set to 0 when successfully executed and 127 when the *command* fails.

Example (Linux specific program):

```
$lastline = exec('cal', $output, $return);
echo '<pre>'; // For better formatting of print_r()
print_r($output);
var_dump($lastline, $return);
```

```
Array
(
  [0] =>      March 2008
  [1] => Su Mo Tu We Th Fr Sa
  [2] =>                    1
  [3] =>  2  3  4  5  6  7  8
```

```
    [4] =>  9 10 11 12 13 14 15
    [5] => 16 17 18 19 20 21 22
    [6] => 23 24 25 26 27 28 29
    [7] => 30 31
)
string(5) "30 31"
int(0)
```

header($string [, *replace_flag*] [, *http_response_code*])

replace_flag – [optional] **$boolean** *default:* TRUE, replace similar header
http_response_code – [optional] **$integer**

Sends an HTTP header specified as **$string**.
Note: Header() *must be used prior to any other output is sent to the user/browser. Use* ***ob_start()*** *to workaround this.*

Examples:

```
header('Location: http://www.someotherplace.com');
```

```
// Redirects the user to the provided URL
```

```
header('HTTP/1.0 404 Not Found');
```

```
// Sends the HTTP status code 404
```

See Also:

ob_start() – Start the output buffer

Classes & Object Oriented PHP

While this is outside of the scope of this book, I have included a few notes here on basic usage to extend the flexibility of this book.

Class Structure: (brackets[] delineate optional syntax)

```
class class_name [extends base_class]{
    var variable_name; // Defines a variable
    function function_name([arguments]) {
        // Stuff to do goes here
    }
}
```

Refer to the containing class – use the reserved variable **$this**

Declare a class: `$variable = new class_name();`

Creating an object: `$variable->function_name();`

Static call to an object: `class_name::function_name();`

Operators

When comparing or processing variables and other values you use operators. Without them, PHP would be more of a word jumble instead of a language. In some unique cases, operators slightly alter the relationship between two variables or their function within PHP. Without further adieu, here they are.

Basic Operators

Add (+): `$a = 1; $a = $a + 5; // $a is equal to 6`
Subtract (-): `$s = 10; $s = $s - 5; // $s is equal to 5`
Multiply (*): `$m = 2; $m = $m * 10; // $m is equal to 20`
Divide (/): `$d = 20; $d = $d / 5; // $d is equal to 4`
Modulus (%) Provides the remainder after division:
`$u = 5; $u = $u % 2; // $u is equal to 1`

Assignment Operators

Add (+=): `$a = 1; $a += 5; // $a is equal to 6`
Subtract (-=): `$s = 10; $s -= 5; // $s is equal to 5`
Multiply (*=): `$m = 2; $m *= 10; // $m is equal to 20`
Divide (/=): `$d = 20; $d /= 5; // $d is equal to 4`
Modulus (%=) Provides the remainder after division:
`$u = 5; $u %= 2; // $u is equal to 1`

Concatenate (.=) Join onto the end of a string:
`$c = 5; $c .= 2; // $c is now a string, '52'`

See Also:

Concatenate – Join together in succession

Comparison Operators

Greater Than (>): `2 > 1`
Less Than (<): `1 < 2`
Greater Than or Equal To (>=): `2 >= 2` `3 >= 2`
Less Than or Equal To (<=): `2 <= 2` `2 <= 3`

Short-Hand Plus or Minus one

Also known as:
Increment (**$integer++;**)
Decrement (**$integer--;**)

Example:

```
$a = 1;
$a = $a + 1; // $a is now equal to 2
$a++; // $a is now equal to 3
$a--; // $a is now equal to 2 again, same as $a = $a - 1;
```

@ - Suppress Errors

Placing the commercial at symbol (@) before a function tells PHP to suppress any errors generated by that function.

Examples:

```
include('DoesNotExist.txt');
```

```
Warning: include(DoesNotExist.txt) [function.include]: failed to open
stream: No such file or directory
```

```
@include('DoesNotExist.txt');
// blank output below because the error was suppressed
```

& - Pass by Reference

References allow two variables to refer to the same content. In other words, a variable points to its content (rather than becoming that content). Passing by reference allows two variables to point to the same content under different names. The ampersand (&) is placed before the variable to be referenced.

Examples:

```
$a = 1;
$b = &$a; // $b references the same value as $a, currently 1
$b = $b + 1; // 1 is added to $b, which effects $a the same way
echo "b is equal to $b, and a is equal to $a";
```

```
b is equal to 2, and a is equal to 2
```

♣ ♣ ♣

Use this for functions when you wish to simply alter the original variable and return it again to the same variable name with its new value assigned.

```
function add(&$var){ // The & is before the argument $var
  $var++;
}
$a = 1;
$b = 10;
add($a);
echo "a is $a,";
add($b);
echo " a is $a, and b is $b"; // Note: $a and $b are NOT referenced
```

```
a is 2, a is 2, and b is 11
```

You can also do this to alter an array with foreach:

```
$array = array(1,2,3,4);
foreach ($array as &$value){
    $value = $value + 10;
}
unset ($value); // Must be included, $value remains after foreach loop
print_r($array);
```

```
Array ( [0] => 11 [1] => 12 [2] => 13 [3] => 14 )
```

Ternary Operator

The Ternary Operator is a short-hand form for evaluating what to do when an *expression* is evaluated as either TRUE or FALSE. The conditional returns either the TRUE or FALSE output. Basic format is as follows:

```
(expr) ? ValueIfTrue : ValueIfFalse ;
```

Examples:

```
$boolean = TRUE;
$result = ($boolean) ? 'Is True' : 'Is False';
echo $result;
```

```
Is True
```

```
// $result is not yet set
$result = (isset($result)) ? $result+1 : 10;
echo " \$result = $result.";
$result = (isset($result)) ? $result+1 : 10;
echo " \$result = $result.";
```

```
$result = 10. $result = 11.
```

The Equal Sign

Assignment (=): Assigns the value on the right to the variable on the left
Equality (==): Checks if the left and right values are equal
Identical (===): Checks if the left and right values are equal AND identical

Example:

```
$a = 1; // Sets the value of $a as 1 by assignment
$b = TRUE; // Sets the value of $b to the boolean TRUE
if ($a == $b){
    echo 'a is equal to b.';
}
if ($a === $b){
    echo 'a is identical and equal to b.';
}
```

```
a is equal to b.
```

Not (!), Not Equal to (!=), Not Identical to (!==)

Used in conditional statements to evaluate as true a FALSE result of an *expression* or if a value is NOT equal to the second value.

Example:

```
$a = 1;
if (!isset($a)){ // If the variable $a is NOT set then...
    echo '$a is not set'; // The expression is TRUE if it is NOT set
    // Since there is no ELSE statement, nothing is displayed
}
if ($a != 0){
    echo '$a does not equal zero';
}
```

```
$a does not equal zero
```

*See **The Equal Sign** above for equality versus identical*

Concatenate (The Period)

A period is used to join dissimilar items as part of a string in the same order as they are listed. In many cases this is used to reference the value of a function or of an array, which cannot be referenced within double quotations ("") when being assigned to a **$string** variable.

Example:

```
$array = array( 1 => 'Hello' );
$string = 'World';
echo '$string in single quotes, followed by ' . $array[1] . "$string";
```

```
$string in single quotes, followed by HelloWorld
```

Comparison Operators (non-arithmetic)

and (&&)
or (||)
xor (xor) - Or, but not All

Examples:

```
if (1 == 1 && 2 == 2){
    echo 'And is True';
}
```

```
And is True
```

```
if (1 == 1 || 2 == 2){
    echo 'At least one of these is True';
}
```

```
At least one of these is True
```

```
if (1 == 1 xor 2 == 10){
    echo 'One of these is True, but not both';
}
```

```
One of these is True, but not both
```

Control Structures

The heart of PHP is the control structures. Variables and arrays are lonely without them as they facilitate comparisons, loops, and large hands telling you to go that way and do it this way. Okay, I made that last part up. Here we go!

If, ElseIf, Else

```
if (expr) {
    // If expr is TRUE,  do this, then exit the IF loop
  }elseif (expr2) {
    // If expr is FALSE, and expr2 is TRUE, do this, then exit the loop
  }else{
    // If all expr's are FALSE, do this, then exit
}
```

There can be only one instance of *else* in an *if* statement, but multiple *elseif* expressions are allowed prior to the *else* statement.

Example:

```
$x = 1;
if ($x < 1){
    echo '$x is less than 1';
  }elseif ($x == 1){ // Note the double equals, for comparison
    echo '$x is equal to 1';
  }else{
    echo '$x is neither equal to 1 or less than 1';
}
```

```
$x is equal to 1
```

See Also:

switch – A simpler, more organized usage than multiple if/elseIf combinations
break – Stops a loop and exits regardless of if the statement evaluates as true

♣ ♣ ♣

Alternative syntax for an *if* statement:

```
if (expr):
    // If expr is TRUE,  do this, then exit the IF loop
  elseif (expr2):
    // If expr is FALSE, and expr2 is TRUE, do this, then exit the
loop
  else:
    // If all expr's are FALSE, do this, then exit
endif;
```

Switch

```
switch (expr) {
  case value:
    // Do this if value matches
    break;
  case value2:
    // Do this if value2 matches
    break;
  default:     // [optional]
    // Do this if no other cases match. Does not have to be at the end
    break;
}
```

expr – A **$string**, **$integer**, or **$float** to be compared against

A *switch* evaluates the *expr* against any number of *cases* or options, specifying the behavior for each *case*.

Cases can be 'stacked' to allow the same portion of code to be evaluated for different cases:

```
switch (expr) {
  case value:
  case value2:
    // Do this if value or value2 matches
}
```

The *switch* is evaluated line-by-line, and therefore if there was no **break** command, the *case* declaration would effectively be ignored and the code would continue to be processed until the *switch* ends or a *break;* is reached.

```
$x = 1;
switch ($x) {
  case 1:
    echo '1'; // Note the lack of a break;
  case 2:
    echo '2'; // Without the break, this is processed line-by-line
}
```

12

Finally, the *default* statement is optional, but defines what to do if no cases are matched. It can be used in troubleshooting to identify when you failed to include a case for an expected output.

Examples:

```
$x = 2;
switch ($x) {
  case 1:
    echo '1';
    break;
  case 2:
    echo '2';
    break;
  case 3:
    echo '3';
    break;
}
```

```
2
```

```
$x = 'howdy';
switch ($x) {
  case 'hi':
    echo 'Hi there';
    break;
  default: // Can be anywhere, all cases evaluated before it is used
    echo 'Greetings';
    break;
  case 'hello':
    echo 'Hello there';
    break;
}
```

```
Greetings
```

See Also:

break – Stops a loop and exits regardless of if the statement evaluates as true

Alternative syntax for a *switch* statement:

```
switch (expr):
  case value:
    // Do this if value matches
    break;
  case value2:
    // Do this if value2 matches
    break;
  default:     // [optional]
    // Do this if no other cases match. Does not have to be at the end
    break;
endswitch;
```

while

```
while (expr) {
    // If expr is TRUE,  do this, then evaluate expr again
}
```

The *while* loop checks the *expr* and if it evaluates as true, the script runs through the entire contents of the *while* until it finishes, then it evaluates the *expr* again and repeats until the *expr* evaluates as false.

Example:

```
$x = 1;
while ($x <= 3){
    echo "$x, ";
    $x++; // increments $x by adding 1. Short-hand version
}
```

```
1, 2, 3,
```

See Also:

do-while – Same as *while,* except the *expr* is evaluated after the first action
break – Stops a loop and exits regardless of a TRUE statement evaluation
continue – Stops the iteration of the loop, and the *expr* is evaluated again

Alternative syntax for a *while* statement:

```
while (expr):
    // If expr is TRUE,  do this, then evaluate expr again
endwhile;
```

do-while

```
do {
  // Do this
} while (expr);
```

The *do-while* loop performs whatever is inside the *do* statement, checks the *expr,* then if it evaluates as TRUE, runs through the entire contents of the *do* until it finishes, evaluating the *expr* again, and repeating until the *expr* evaluates as FALSE.

Example:

```
$x = 1;
do {
    echo "$x, ";
    $x++; // Makes $x = 2, therefore the while will evaluate as false
  } while ($x <= 1);
```

```
1,
```

See Also:

while – Similar to *do-while,* except the *expr* is evaluated first
break – Stops a loop and exits regardless of if the statement evaluates as true
continue – Stops the iteration of the loop, and the *expr* is evaluated again

for

```
for (expr1; expr2; expr3) {
    // If expr2 is TRUE, do this
}
```

When started, the *for* loop executes *expr1* once at the beginning. Next, *expr2* is evaluated. If *expr2* is true, the code inside the *for* loop is executed. When the *for* loop reaches the end, *expr3* is executed before looping and checking *expr2* again.

Example:

```
for ($x = 1; $x <= 5; $x++){
    echo $x;
}
```

```
12345
```

See Also:

break – Stops the *for* loop and exits it immediately
continue – Stops the current iteration of the *for* loop, and *expr3* is executed before checking *expr2* again

Alternative syntax for a *for* statement:

```
for (expr1; expr2; expr3):
    // If expr2 is TRUE, do this
endfor;
```

An example of **continue** and **break** in a *for* loop:

```
for ($v=0;$v<=10;$v++){
  echo $v;
    if ($v == 5){
      continue;
    }
    if ($v == 8){
      break;
    }
  echo ',';
}
```

```
0,1,2,3,4,56,7,8
```

foreach

```
foreach ($array as $value){
    // Do something
}
// Another form, for keys and values
foreach ($array as $key => $value){
    // Do something
}
```

The *foreach* loop goes through all items in an array, assigning a temporary variable name for *value* and, if chosen, the *key* as well so they can be used within the executed code inside the loop.

Examples:

```
$array = array('John' => 20, 'Jane' => 24, 'Joseph' => 28);
foreach ($array as $value){
    echo "$value, ";
}
```

```
20, 24, 28,
```

```
foreach ($array as $name => $age){
    echo "$name - $age";
    echo '<br />'; // XHTML for a line break
}
```

```
John - 20
Jane - 24
Joseph - 28
```

See Also:

Pass by Reference – Using the ampersand (&) to alter an array through *foreach*

break [$integer]

$integer – [optional] Specifies the number of nested loops to break out of

Exits and stops execution of the current (default) *for, foreach, while, do-while,* or *switch* loop.

Example:

```
$counter = 0;
while (1 == 1){ // Will run forever
    while (0 == 0){ // Will also run forever
        $counter++; // Increment $counter plus 1
        echo $counter;
        if ($counter == 5){
          break 2;
        }
    }
    echo 'First while loop'; // Never displayed because of break 2;
    break; // Never run, but if it did, would end the first while loop
}
```

```
12345
```

continue [$integer]

$integer – [optional] Specifies the number of nested loops to skip out of
Note: *The **$integer** does not supply the number of iterations to skip, it always only stops the current iteration from continuing any further.*

Skips the rest of the current loop iteration and if applicable, continues to the next iteration of the loop[3].

Example:

```
for ($x=1;$x<=10;$x++){
    if ($x == 5){
      continue;
    }   // The echo never occurs if $x == 5
    echo $x;
}
```

```
1234678910
```

return [$variable]

$variable – [optional] The variable to be returned from a function

If used as part of a regular script and not part of a function, it works the same as **exit()** or **die()**. Return is more commonly used as part of a function to assign a value to the results of a function back at the original function call.

See Also:

Functions – Provides an example of returning a **$variable** as part of a function
exit() – Terminate the current script immediately

include(*file*)

file - **$string**

Include and evaluate the *file* as part of the current script/page. This is an easy way to store common variables, functions[4], or lines of HTML that will be included by multiple scripts/pages. Failure of the function generates an error.

Example:

```
include('somefile.inc');
```

---

3 In the case of a *switch*, **continue** has the same effect as **break**

4 Functions should only be included once. Consider using **include_once()** or **require_once()**

include_once(*file*)

file - **$string**

Include and evaluate the *file* as part of the current script/page. If the file has already been included, it will ignore the request. This is an easy way to store common variables, functions, or lines of HTML that will be included by multiple scripts/pages.
Failure of the function generates an error and terminates the script immediately.

Example:

```
include_once('somefile.php');
```

require(*file*)

file - **$string**

Include and evaluate the *file* as part of the current script/page. This is an easy way to store common variables, functions[5], or lines of HTML that will be included by multiple scripts/pages. Failure of the function generates an error.

Example:

```
require('somefile.htm');
```

require_once(*file*)

file - **$string**

Include and evaluate the *file* as part of the current script/page. If the file has already been included, it will ignore the request. This is an easy way to store common variables, functions, or lines of HTML that will be included by multiple scripts/pages.
Failure of the function generates an error and terminates the script immediately.

Example:

```
require_once('somefile.php');
```

5 Functions should only be included once. Consider using **require_once()**

Global Variables

While some global variables can be created through the use of **define()**, some are reserved because of a special function, giving access to different types of data. All global variables listed below are arrays that may or may not contain data, depending on the current script and environment.

$_SERVER

$_SERVER['HTTP_USER_AGENT'] – Browser description from header

```
[HTTP_USER_AGENT] => Mozilla/5.0 (X11; U; Linux i686; en-US; rv:
1.8.1.12) Gecko/20080207 Ubuntu/7.10 (gutsy) Firefox/2.0.0.12
```

$_SERVER['HTTP_REFERER'] – The page address that referred the user

```
[HTTP_REFERER] => http://www.example.com/index.htm
```

$_SERVER['REMOTE_ADDR'] – The client's IP address

```
[REMOTE_ADDR] => 127.0.0.1
```

$_SERVER['DOCUMENT_ROOT'] – System root location of current script

```
[DOCUMENT_ROOT] => /opt/lampp/htdocs
```

$_SERVER['SCRIPT_FILENAME'] – Absolute path of current script

```
[SCRIPT_FILENAME] => /opt/lampp/htdocs/test.php
```

$_SERVER['REQUEST_URI'] – The Universal Resource Identifier for the page

```
[REQUEST_URI] => /test.php?test=value
```

$_SERVER['SCRIPT_NAME'] – The current scripts path

```
[SCRIPT_NAME] => /test.php
```

$_SERVER['QUERY_STRING'] – The current scripts path

```
[QUERY_STRING] => test=value
```

$_SERVER['PHP_SELF'] – The name of the current script, relative to the root

```
[PHP_SELF] => /test.php
```

♣ ♣ ♣

When submitting a form to the same page/file that contains it, you can use the $_SERVER['PHP_SELF'] variable to dynamically provide the location.

```
<form method="POST" action="<?php echo $SERVER['PHP_SELF']; ?>">
<form method="POST" action="filename.php">
```

$_REQUEST

Includes all variables provided by **$_GET**, **$_POST**, and **$_COOKIE**

$_POST

Includes all variables submitted through HTTP POST, such as an HTML form with action="post".

$_GET

Includes all variables submitted through the query string, either manually or from a form with action="get".

```
http://www.example.com/test.php?query=value
```

```
// Output of print_r($_GET) of the above URL example
Array ( [query] => value )
```

$_SESSION

Variables assigned to the current session.

$_COOKIE

Any cookies stored for the current website. Only visible after the page was reloaded if it was just set using **setcookie()**.

See Also:

setcookie() – Assigning and deleting cookies

$_FILES

Variables provided to the script via POST uploads.

$_ENV

A collection of variables about the server environment.

$GLOBALS

Contains a reference for all variables, global or otherwise, in the script.

Variable Functions

The following functions check details about variables themselves, rather than addressing a specific aspect of a *type* of variable. Put another way, you don't want to know what type of elephant you have, just that it is an elephant, and it is about to trample you. Too much? Oh well, here we go again.

empty($variable)

Determine whether the **$variable** is empty. Returns TRUE if the **$variable** is:

- '' – Empty **$string**
- 0 – For an **$integer**
- '0' – For a **$string**
- array() – For an **$array**
- NULL
- FALSE
- An undeclared variable

Example:

```
$string = 'Hello';
$array = array();
var_dump( empty($string), empty($array), empty($DoesNotExist) );
```

```
bool(false) bool(true) bool(true)
```

See Also:

is_null() – Check whether a variable is NULL
isset() – Check whether a variable has been set/created/declared

is_null($variable)

Determine whether the **$variable** is NULL. Returns TRUE if it is NULL.
***Note:** An undeclared **$variable** will return TRUE but may return an error.*

Example:

```
$string = '';
$integer = 0;
$array = NULL;
var_dump( is_null($string), is_null($integer), is_null($array) );
```

```
bool(false) bool(false) bool(true)
```

isset($variable [, ...$variable...])

*Accepts multiple **$variables** separated by commas, but will only return TRUE if all variables are set*

Determine whether **$variable** has been set/created/declared.

Example:

```
$string = '';
$integer = 0;
var_dump( isset($string,$integer) ); // True because BOTH are set
echo '<br />'; // XHTML break for new line
unset($string); // unset or destroy the variable
var_dump( isset($string), isset($integer) );
```

```
bool(true)
bool(false) bool(true)
```

See Also:

unset() – Destroy/delete a variable or multiple variables

unset($variable [, ...$variable...])

*Accepts multiple **$variables** separated by commas*

Unsets or destroys/deletes the given **$variable**(s).

Example:

```
$string = 'hello';
var_dump( isset($string) ); // Check if it is set
echo '<br />'; // XHTML break for new line
unset($string);
var_dump( isset($string) ); // Check again
```

```
bool(true)
bool(false)
```

See Also:

isset() – Determine whether a variable has been set

is_array($variable)

Determine whether the **$variable** is an array. Returns TRUE if it is an array.

Example:

```
$array = array();
$array2 = array( 'one', 'two', 'three' );
var_dump( is_array($array), is_array($array2) );
```

```
bool(true) bool(true)
```

is_int($variable)

Also known as: **is_integer()**

Determine whether the **$variable** is an integer. Returns TRUE if it is an integer.

Example:

```
$int = 0;
$string = '0';
var_dump( is_int($int), is_int($string) );
```

```
bool(true) bool(false)
```

is_string($variable)

Determine whether the **$variable** is a string. Returns TRUE if it is a string.

Example:

```
$int = 0;
$string = '0';
var_dump( is_string($int), is_string($string) );
```

```
bool(false) bool(true)
```

is_numeric($variable)

Determine whether the **$variable** is an integer or a numeric string (*e.g.* "12"). If either is true, it will return TRUE.

Example:

```
$int = 10;
$string = '10';
var_dump( is_numeric($int), is_numeric($string) );
```

```
bool(true) bool(true)
```

See Also:

is_int() – Determine if a variable is an integer
is_string() – Determine if a variable is an string

var_dump(*expr* [, ...*expr*...])

Accepts multiple expressions, separated by commas
expr – A **$variable** or any expression that generates a result

Shows the type of variable and its value in the following format:

```
type(value)  // When evaluating a boolean, integer, or float
string(length) value  // When evaluating a string
array(length) { value }  // When evaluating an array
```

Example:

```
$integer = 10;
$string = 'Hello';
$array = array( 'one' );
var_dump( $integer, $string, $array, is_string($string) );
```

```
int(10) string(5) "Hello" array(1) { [0]=> string(3) "one" } bool(true)
```

See Also:

echo – Prints the value of a **$scalar**

Surrounding the *var_dump()* with the HTML tags **<pre> </pre>** will present the output of multiple expressions in a more human readable format.

```
// Using the same variables as above
echo '<pre>';
var_dump( $integer, $string, $array, is_string($string) );
echo '</pre>';
```

```
int(10)
string(5) "Hello"
array(1) {
  [0]=>
  string(3) "one"
}
bool(true)
```

print_r($variable)

Output the contents of **$variable**[6]. Typically used to display the contents of an array.

Example:

```
$array = array( 'Apple', 'Orange', 'Melon' );
print_r($array);
```

```
Array ( [0] => Apple [1] => Orange [2] => Melon )
```

See Also:

echo – Display the value of a **$scalar**

6 If $variable is **boolean**, TRUE will output 1, and FALSE will output nothing

If you add the HTML tags **<pre> </pre>** around the output, formatting will be easier to follow.

```
$array = array( 'Apple', 'Orange', 'Melon' );
echo '<pre>';
print_r($array);
echo '</pre>';
```

```
Array
(
 [0] => Apple
 [1] => Orange
 [2] => Melon
)
```

Here is a quick function to do this easily:

```
function preprint($array){
    echo '<pre>'; print_r ($array); echo '</pre>';
}
```

serialize(*value*)

Converts the *value* to a storable representation in a **$string**.

Example:

```
$array = array( 'one', 'two', 'three' );
$output = serialize($array);
echo $output;
```

```
a:3:{i:0;s:3:"one";i:1;s:3:"two";i:2;s:5:"three";}
```

See Also:

unserialize() – Convert a serialized string back into its original *value*

If adding the serialized data to a MySQL database, you will need to escape some characters using **addslashes()** and then remove them again with **stripslashes()** when recovering the value from the database.

```
$array = array( 'one', 'two', 'three' );
$db_ready = addslashes(serialize($array));
// add $db_ready to your database (code not included here)
// retrieve it from the database (code not included here)
$normal = unserialize(stripslashes($db_ready));
```

unserialize($string)

Converts a serialized **$string** back into its original *value*.

Example:

```
$array = array( 'one', 'two', 'three' );
$output = serialize($array);
echo '<pre>';
var_dump($output);
print_r( unserialize($output) );
echo '</pre>';
```

```
string(50) "a:3:{i:0;s:3:"one";i:1;s:3:"two";i:2;s:5:"three";}"
Array
(
    [0] => one
    [1] => two
    [2] => three
)
```

See Also:

serialize() – Convert a *value* to a storable representation in a **$string**

floatval($scalar)

Returns the float value of the **$scalar**.
Note: *If the* ***$scalar*** *is a string starting with integers, characters after the integers will be stripped out.*

Example:

```
$float = 1.34;
$string = "145the words";
$string2 = "0025";
var_dump ( floatval($float), floatval($string), floatval($string2) );
```

```
float(1.34) float(145) float(25)
```

As in the example above, if a string starts with integers and has trailing characters, you can convert this to a float with this command. However, if you intend to use this function to retrieve the string equivalent, any leading zeros will be erased. Be careful!

String Functions

If you were a cat, string functions would be the cat's meow, all puns intended. Besides being a large part of your PHP code, they provide much of the functionality to identify and alter your data into other formats, such as arrays.

addslashes($string)

Adds backslashes (escape string) to items within **$string** to make it safe for database queries. Effects single quotes ('), double quotes ("), backslashes (\ ), and the NUL byte.

Example:

```
$string = ' Tom said, "Marcus is mad!"';
echo $string;
$string = addslashes($string);
echo $string;
```

```
Tom said, "Marcus is mad!" Tom said, \"Marcus is mad!\"
```

See Also:

get_magic_quotes_gpc – Server setting for automatically applying addslashes to GET/POST/COOKIE data
stripslashes() – Remove the backslashes created by **addslashes()**

stripslashes($string)

Removes backslashes (escape string) from items within **$string** added through **addslashes()** or **magic_quotes_gpc**.

Example:

```
$string = ' Tom said, "Marcus is mad!"';
$string = addslashes($string);
echo $string;
$string = stripslashes($string);
echo $string;
```

```
Tom said, \"Marcus is mad!\" Tom said, "Marcus is mad!"
```

See Also:

get_magic_quotes_gpc – Server setting for automatically applying addslashes to GET/POST/COOKIE data
addslashes() – Adds backslashes to make a string safe for database queries

chunk_split($string [, *length*] [, *endstring*])

length – [optional] **$integer** *default*: 76
endstring – [optional] **$string** *default*: "\r\n" (carriage return and new line)

Splits **$string** into sections of *length* characters, every section is terminated with the *endstring*. Evaluates only the character length to generate the resulting string.

Example:

```
$string = 'Hello Nurse!';
$string = chunk_split($string, 3);
var_dump($string);
echo nl2br($string); // Converts \n to the XHTML <br />
echo 'Notice I am on a new line?';
```

```
string(20) "Hel lo Nur se! " Hel
lo
Nur
se!
Notice I am on a new line?
```

HTML source code:

```
string(20) "Hel
lo
Nur
se!
"
Hel<br />
lo <br />
Nur<br />
se!<br />
Notice I am on a new line?
```

See Also:

nl2br() – Convert instances of \n into the XHTML <br /> line break
str_replace() – Replace specified characters in a string
wordwrap() – Similar to **chunk_split()**, but with some minor variations

> The \r\n are formatting characters, which are ignored in HTML if part of the standard output. If placed within <textarea> or <pre> (preformatted) tags, they are evaluated properly in the browser's output.

```
$string = 'Hello Nurse!';
$string = chunk_split($string, 3);
echo '<pre>';
echo $string;
echo '</pre>';
```

```
Hel
lo 
Nur
se!
```

wordwrap($string [, *length*] [, *breakstring*] [, *wordcut*])

length – [optional] **$integer** *default*: 75
breakstring – [optional] **$string** *default*: "\n" (new line)
wordcut – [optional] **$boolean** *default*: FALSE, words are not broken up

Splits **$string** into sections of *length* characters with the *breakstring*. If *wordcut* is set to TRUE, words longer than the specified *length* will be split, ensuring the exact width.

Examples:

```
$origstring = 'I said to her, Hellooooo Nurse!!!';
$string = wordwrap($origstring, 8);
echo nl2br($string); // Converts \n to the XHTML <br />
```

```
I said
to her,
Hellooooo
Nurse!!!
```

```
$origstring = 'I said to her, Hellooooo Nurse!!!';
$string = wordwrap($origstring, 8, "<BR \>\n", TRUE);
echo $string;
```

```
I said
to her,
Helloooo
o
Nurse!!!
```

See Also:

nl2br() – Convert instances of \n into the XHTML <br /> line break
str_replace() – Replace specified characters in a string
chunk_split() – Similar to **wordwrap()**, but with some minor variations

For standards compliance, sending text based email with the **mail()** command should have the message parsed with **wordwrap()** prior to being supplied to **mail()**.

count_chars($string [, *mode*])

mode – [optional] **$integer** (0, 1, 2, 3, or 4) *default:* 0

Values: 0 – Returns an array with the count for all characters
1 – Returns an array with the count for all characters with at least one instance in **$string**
2 – Returns an array with the count for all characters with zero instances
3 – Returns a string of all characters contained within **$string**
4 – Returns a string of all characters not contained within **$string**

Checks **$string** for instances of all ASCII characters and counts the number of times that a character is included within the string. Output varies depending on *mode*.
Note: *The key in the array is the ASCII byte-value of the character (modes 0-2) while the string output is the characters themselves (modes 3 and 4).*

Examples:

```
$string = 'Hello';
$array = count_chars($string, 1);
echo '<pre>'; // Not required, included for easier readability
print_r($array);
```

```
Array
(
    [72] => 1
    [101] => 1
    [108] => 2
    [111] => 1
)
```

```
foreach ($array as $key => $value){
    $char = chr($key); // Character represented by the byte-value
    $chararray[$char] = $value; // Make new array with characters
}
print_r($chararray);
```

```
Array
(
    [H] => 1
    [e] => 1
    [l] => 2
    [o] => 1
)
```

```
$usedcharacters = count_chars($string, 3);
var_dump($usedcharacters);
```

```
string(4) "Helo"
```

See Also:

chr() – Get the ASCII character represented by its byte-value

chr($integer)

$integer – 0 - 255

Returns the single character string representation of the ASCII byte-value (**$integer)**

Example:

```
echo chr(72);
```

```
H
```

echo *argument* [, *...argument...*]

Accepts multiple arguments separated by a comma
argument – A **$scalar** or function with scalar output[7]

Outputs the value of the *argument* to the user.

Example:

```
echo 'Hello';
```

```
Hello
```

print *argument*

argument – A **$scalar** or function with scalar output[7]

Outputs the value of the *argument* to the user, always returns 1. Use **echo()** instead.

Example:

```
$x = print 'Hello';
print $x;
```

```
Hello
```

explode(*delimiter*, $string [, *limit*])

delimiter – **$string**, if set to '', explode will return FALSE
limit – [optional] **$integer**, *default:* no limit

Returns an array of strings created by searching through **$string** and separating it by using the provided *delimiter* as the separation point. *Limit* sets the maximum number of elements, with the last element of the array being the remainder of the string[8].

7 $boolean is represented by 1 (TRUE) or nothing (FALSE) while floats may be displayed as integers at greater than e6

8 If *limit* is negative, all values are returned except the last *limit* number of them

Example:

```
$explodeme = '02-01-1980';
$array = explode('-', $explodeme); // dash (-) is the delimiter
echo '<pre>'; // For easier readability
print_r($array);
```

```
Array
(
    [0] => 02
    [1] => 01
    [2] => 1980
)
```

```
$array = explode('-', $explodeme, 2); // Limit to 2 elements
print_r($array);
```

```
Array
(
    [0] => 02
    [1] => 01-1980
)
```

See Also:

implode() – Creates a string from array elements, using a joining string

As shown above, explode can be used to break apart common language syntax, such as separating a paragraph submitted by a user into its individual sentences, or allowing a user to submit tags for a particular item, separated by commas, and then **explode()** those items for database storage.

implode(*limiter*, $array)

limiter – **$string**

Returns a string containing the contents of **$array** joined by the provided *limiter*.

Example:

```
$array = array( 'Hello', 'World', '!' );
$string = implode(' ', $array); // Using a space as the limiter
echo $string;
```

```
Hello World !
```

See Also:

explode() – Separate a string into an array using a specific delimiting string

sprintf(*formatting, inputs* [, *...inputs...*]

Accepts multiple inputs to be used when specified in formatting

formatting – **$string**, specific formatting string, explained below
inputs – **$scalar**(s) to be formatted

Returns a formatted string *formatting*, using the *inputs* to dynamically input their values into the formatted string using a preset set of rules, specified below.

The following is the available nomenclature for the *formatting* input.

Every time an input is expected to be used and evaluated as part of the formatted string, it is preceded by a percent sign (%), followed by the specifiers/rules:
Note: *All specifiers, excluding the* ***type*** *specifier, are optional.*

- A **sign** specifier. Placing a plus sign (+) forces negative AND positive signs to be visible (only negative values are specified by default).
- A **padding** specifier. The default is a space, and does not need to be specified. A zero (0) can be used as well without any secondary notation. If any other character is to be used, it should be preceded with a single quote (').
- An **alignment** specifier. The default is right-justified (thus padding is placed on the left of the string). Placing a dash/subtract (-) will set it to left-justified.
- A **width** specifier. This integer determines the minimum length in characters the output should be. When combined with padding, the specified width minus the input's length determines the number of padded characters that will be added.
- A **precision** specifier. A period (.) followed by an integer, sets the number of decimal places that should be output for a float. If used on a string, it sets a maximum character limit for the output.
- A **type** specifier:
  - % - a literal percent sign, thus would be written %% to display a percent sign in the formatting string
  - *b* – the input should be an integer, a binary number is the output.

- *c* - the input should be an integer between 0-255, representing the ASCII byte-value. The character represented is output.
- *d* – the input should be an integer.
- *e* – the input is scientific notation.
- *u* – the input is an unsigned decimal number.
- *f* – the input is a float (locale aware).
- *F* - the input is a float (not locale aware).
- *o* – the input is an integer, an octal number is the output.
- *s* – the input is a string.
- *x* - the input is an integer, a hexadecimal number is the output (with lowercase letters).
- *X* - the input is an integer, a hexadecimal number is the output (with uppercase letters).

Examples:

Basic substitution, no optional specifiers

```
$string = 'cat';
$integer = 10;
echo sprintf("I have %d %s(s)", $integer, $string);
```

```
I have 10 cat(s)
```

Basic substitution, type specification automatic adjustments

```
$string = 'cat';
$string2 = '10 blah';
echo sprintf("I have %d %s(s)", $string2, $string);
```

```
I have 10 cat(s)
```

Using the **sign** specifier

```
$string = 'cat';
$integer = '10';
echo sprintf("Dagger has a %+d against %ss", $integer, $string);
```

```
Dagger has a +10 against cats
```

Using **padding** and **width** specifiers (default **padding** specifier of a space)

```
$string = 'cat'; // length, 3 characters
echo '<pre>'; // HTML Required to display the formating properly
echo sprintf("3 spaces added: |%6s", $string);
  // Used padding of 6 characters, 6 - 3 = 3 spaces padded
```

```
Pad from line 3 spaces: |    cat
```

Using **padding** and **width** using a zero (0) for padding

```
$month = 12;
$day = 1;
$year = 1980;
echo sprintf (" Date: %02d/%02d/%04d.", $month, $day, $year);
$year = 80;
echo sprintf (" Date: %02d/%02d/%04d.", $month, $day, $year);
```

```
Date: 12/01/1980. Date: 12/01/0080.
```

Using **padding** and **width** using a custom character, the asterisk (*)

```
$endofpassword = 'word';
$output = sprintf("Your password: %'*8s", $endofpassword);
echo $output;
```

```
Your password: ****word
```

Using **padding**, **alignment** (left), and **width**

```
$endofpassword = 'word';
$output = sprintf("Your password: %'*-8s", $endofpassword);
echo $output;
```

```
Your password: word****
```

Using the **precision** specifier

```
$scientific = 1.2e3;
echo sprintf("Three decimal places: %.3e", $scientific);
```

```
Three decimal places: 1.200e+3
```

```
$float = 1.2e3;
echo sprintf("Two decimal places: %.2f", $float);
```

```
Two decimal places: 1200.00
```

```
$string = 'Hello World!';
echo sprintf("Cut-off after 4 characters: %.4s", $string);
```

```
Cut-off after 4 characters: Hell
```

See Also:

printf() – prints a formatted string results rather than simply returning them
sscanf() – Parses a string through a formatted string, reverse of **sprintf()**

For MySQL security, you can use **sprintf()** to force user input to have a maximum length and be valid for the structure of your database. Use the **precision** specifier to automatically parse the string submitted by GET or POST.

printf(*formatting, inputs* [, *...inputs...*]

Accepts multiple inputs to be used when specified in formatting

formatting – **$string**, specific formatting string. *See* ***sprintf()*** *for nomenclature*
inputs – **$scalar**(s) to be formatted

Prints a formatted string *formatting*, using the *inputs* to dynamically input their values into the formatted string using a preset set of rules.
Note: *See* ***sprintf()*** *for rules for formatting strings.*

Example:

```
$string = 'puppies';
printf("I think %s are cute.", $string);
```

```
I think puppies are cute.
```

See Also:

sprintf() – Returns the formatted string, explains rules/nomenclature

sscanf($string, *formatting* [, ...*outputs*...]

Accepts multiple [optional] outputs, but changes the behavior of the function

Examines the given **$string** and parses it based on the expected *formatting*. Returns an array when no *outputs* are included. If *outputs* are included, they specify by reference the variable names to assign the formatted contents. ***Note:*** *See* ***sprintf()*** *for rules for formatting strings –* ***type*** *specifiers.*

Examples:

```
$string = '12/1/1980';
$array = sscanf($string, "%d/%d/%d");
echo '<pre>'; // For improved readability
print_r($array);
```

```
Array
(
    [0] => 12
    [1] => 1
    [2] => 1980
)
```

```
$string = '12/1/1980';
$outputs_count = sscanf($string, "%d/%d/%d", $month, $day, $year);
var_dump ($month, $day, $year);
```

```
int(12) int(1) int(1980)
```

See Also:

sprintf() – Reverse of **sscanf()** and provides explanation of formatting strings
list() – Assigns the values of an array to variable names

htmlspecialchars($string [, *quotes_flag*] [, *character_set*])

quotes_flag – [optional] **$string** *default:* ENT_COMPAT (double quotes only)
Other values: ENT_QUOTES (both single and double quotes)
ENT_NOQUOTES (neither double nor single)
character_set – [optional] **$string** *default:* ISO-8859-1

Converts some characters in **$string** with special meaning in HTML to their safe HTML entities. This includes (but may be limited by some optional flags): double quotes ("), single quotes ('), greater than (>), less than (<), and ampersand (&).

Example:

```
$string = '<strong>Hello & World!</strong><br />';
echo htmlspecialchars($string);
```

HTML source code:

```
&lt;strong&gt;Hello &amp; World!&lt;/strong&gt;&lt;br /&gt;
```

See Also:

htmlspecialchars_decode() – Reverses the effect of **htmlspecialchars()**
htmlentities() – Effects all HTML entities, not just the five above

htmlspecialchars_decode($string [, *quotes_flag*])

quotes_flag – [optional] **$string** *default:* ENT_COMPAT (double quotes only)
Other values: ENT_QUOTES (both single and double quotes)
ENT_NOQUOTES (neither double nor single)

Converts HTML entities back to the character representation in **$string**. This includes (but may be limited by some optional flags): double quotes ("), single quotes ('), greater than (>), less than (<), and ampersand (&).

Example:

```
$string = '&lt;strong&gt;Hello &amp; World!';
echo htmlspecialchars_decode($string);
```

HTML source code:

```
<strong>Hello & World!
```

See Also:

htmlspecialchars() – Converts the five items above into their HTML entities
html_entity_decode() – Effects all HTML entities, not just the five above

htmlentities($string [, *quotes_flag*] [, *character_set*])

quotes_flag – [optional] **$string** *default:* ENT_COMPAT (double quotes only)
Other values: ENT_QUOTES (both single and double quotes)
ENT_NOQUOTES (neither double nor single)
character_set – [optional] **$string** *default:* ISO-8859-1

Converts some characters in **$string** with special meaning in HTML to their safe HTML entities. This includes (but may be limited by some optional flags): double quotes ("), single quotes ('), greater than (>), less than (<), and ampersand (&).

Example:

```
$string = "<strong>'Hello World!'";
echo htmlentities($string, ENT_QUOTES);
```

HTML source code:

```
&lt;strong&gt;&#039;Hello World!&#039;
```

See Also:

html_entity_decode() – Reverses the effect of **htmlentities()**
htmlspecialchars() – Effects only five specific HTML entities

html_entity_decode($string [, *quotes_flag*] [, *character_set*])

quotes_flag – [optional] **$string** *default:* ENT_COMPAT (double quotes only)
Other values: ENT_QUOTES (both single and double quotes)
ENT_NOQUOTES (neither double nor single)
character_set – [optional] **$string** *default:* ISO-8859-1

Converts all HTML entities back to the character representation in **$string**.

Example:

```
$string = '&lt;strong&gt;&#039;Hello World!&#039;';
echo html_entity_decode($string); // single quotes not converted
```

HTML source code:

```
<strong>&#039;Hello World!&#039;
```

See Also:

htmlentities() – Converts all HTML entities
htmlspecialchars_decode() – Decodes five specific HTML entities

trim($string [, *characters*])

characters – [optional] **$string**

Remove from the beginning and end of **$string** the following characters when *characters* is not included: whitespace (' '), tab (\t), new line (\n), carriage return (\r), NUL byte (\0), and the vertical tab (\x0B). If *characters* is included, that list is used instead[9].
Note: *Once a character not from the list is reached, trimming halts.*

Examples:

```
$string = "  \n Hello World! \t\t";
echo trim($string);
```

```
Hello World!
```

9 Within *characters*, a double period (..) can specify a range (*e.g.* a..z is a through z)

```
echo trim($string, " \t\n!r");
// r will not be removed because d is not in the list
```

```
Hello World
```

```
echo trim($string, " \t\n!d..r"); // range of d through r (lowercase)
```

```
Hello W
```

See Also:

ltrim() – Trim only from the beginning of the string
rtrim() – Trim only from the end of the string

ltrim($string [, *characters*])

characters – [optional] **$string**

Remove from the beginning of **$string** the following characters when *characters* is not included: whitespace (" "), tab (\t), new line (\n), carriage return (\r), NUL byte (\0), and the vertical tab (\x0B). If *characters* is included, that list is used instead[10].
Note: *Once a character not from the list is reached, trimming halts.*

Examples:

```
$string = "  \n Hello World!";
echo ltrim($string);
```

```
Hello World!
```

```
echo trim($string, " \nA..Ha..z");
// All capital letters between A and H, and all lowercase letters
```

```
World!
```

See Also:

trim() – Trim from the beginning and the end of the string
rtrim() – Trim only from the end of the string

rtrim($string [, *characters*])

Also known as **chop()**
characters – [optional] **$string**

Remove from the end of **$string** the following characters when *characters* is not included: whitespace (" "), tab (\t), new line (\n), carriage return (\r), NUL byte (\0), and the vertical tab (\x0B). If *characters* is included, that list is used instead[10].
Note: *Once a character not from the list is reached, trimming halts.*

10 Within *characters*, a double period (..) can specify a range (*e.g.* a..z is a through z)

Examples:

```
$string = "Hello World42! \t\t";
echo trim($string);
```

```
Hello World42!
```

```
echo trim($string, " \t!0..9");
// Range included is all numbers between 0 and 9
```

```
Hello World
```

See Also:

ltrim() – Trim only from the beginning of the string
trim() – Trim from the beginning and the end of the string

crypt($string [, *salt*])

salt – [optional] **$string**

Performs a one-way hashing encryption on **$string** using an algorithm specified by the system[11]. The *salt* can be used to generate a stronger encryption, but when not specified and generated by the system, it will be created once per run of the script.

Example:

```
$password = 'mypassword';
echo crypt($password); // Output will vary
```

```
$1$QeU8Xekg$KhD/hMl4C9zDpGc2WszeD.
```

See Also:

md5() – MD5 algorithm based encryption, portable, more secure, commonly used
sha1() – Sha1 algorithm based encryption, portable, most secure

md5($string [, *raw_flag*])

raw_flag – [optional] **$boolean** *default:* FALSE, 32-character hexadecimal

Performs a one-way hashing encryption on **$string** using the MD5 Message-Digest Algorithm. If the *raw_flag* is set to TRUE, it returns a raw binary format with a length of 16 characters.

Example:

```
$password = 'mypassword';
echo md5($password);
```

```
34819d7beeabb9260a5c854bc85b3e44
```

11 Software moving between platforms may have different encryptions, and thus will cause problems with compatibility. Best to use **md5()** or **sha1()** instead for portability

See Also:

sha1() – Sha1 algorithm based encryption

For better security in storing user passwords, the use of a salt should be considered. The salt is basically a string added onto the supplied **$string** to increase its length and complexity. In the case of user passwords, it would be randomly created by the system then saved to the database as a separate entry in the database from the password for that user. This helps protect against reverse md5 dictionary attacks.

```
$password = 'password'; // Very bad password
$salt = substr(md5(uniqid(mt_rand(), TRUE)), 0, 5); // 5 char. salt
$salted_password_hash = md5($salt . md5($password));
echo $salted_password_hash; // Output varies
```

```
d1239dcc6e017572ea6fed5df0d6e07e
```

md5_file(*filename* [, *raw_flag*])

filename – **$string**
raw_flag – [optional] **$boolean** *default:* FALSE, 32-character hexadecimal

Generates the MD5 hash of a file with *filename*. If the *raw_flag* is set to TRUE, it returns a raw binary format with a length of 16 characters.

Example:

```
$hash = md5_file('somefile.txt');
```

See Also:

md5() – MD5 algorithm based encryption for a string

sha1($string [, *raw_flag*])

raw_flag – [optional] **$boolean** *default:* FALSE, 40-character hexadecimal

Performs a one-way hashing encryption on **$string** using the US Secure Hash Algorithm. If the raw_flag is set to TRUE, it returns a raw binary format with a length of 20.

Example:

```
$password = 'mypassword';
echo sha1($password);
```

```
91dfd9ddb4198affc5c194cd8ce6d338fde470e2
```

See Also:

md5() – MD5 algorithm based encryption, commonly used

♣ ♣ ♣

Please see **md5()** tip for adding a salt to a password for extra security.

sha1_file(*filename* [, *raw_flag*])

filename – **$string**
raw_flag – [optional] **$boolean** *default:* FALSE, 40-character hexadecimal

Generates the Sha1 hash of a file with *filename*. If the raw_flag is set to TRUE, it returns a raw binary format with a length of 20.

Example:

```
$hash = sha1_file('somefile.txt');
```

See Also:

sha1() – Sha1 algorithm based encryption for a string

number_format($float [, *decimals*] [, *decimal_point, thousand_separator*]

decimals – [optional] **$integer** *default:* 0, no decimal places
decimal_point – [optional] **$string** *default:* period (.)
thousand_separator – [optional] **$string** *default:* comma (,)

Format the **$float** with thousand separating and decimal places, if specified.
Note: *Rounding occurs if the float has more values than the formatting specifies.*

Examples:

```
$float = 1234567.891;
echo number_format($float);
```

```
1,234,568
```

```
echo number_format($float, 2); // US notation
```

```
1,234,567.89
```

```
echo number_format($float, 2, ",", " "); // French formatting
```

```
1 234 567,89
```

nl2br($string)

Replaces all instances of the new line (\n) formatting character in **$string** with the XHTML line break <br />.

Example:

```
$string = "Hello\nWorld";
echo nl2br($string);
```

HTML Source Code:

```
Hello<br />World
```

Standard output:

```
Hello
World
```

parse_str($string [, $array])

Examines **$string** as a query string and assigns the variables with names equal to the query's key, then assigning values equal to the query's value. If **$array** was specified, query variables will be assigned to an array instead with the same key => value association.
Note: *Output is affected by the magic_quotes_gpc setting the same as $_GET.*

Examples:

```
$query_string = 'key=value&color=red';
parse_str($query_string);
echo "\$key equals $key, and \$color equals $color";
```

```
$key equals value, and $color equals red
```

```
$query_string = "key=value&color='red'";
parse_str($query_string, $array);
echo '<pre>'; // For easier readability
print_r($array);
```

Without magic_quotes_gpc enabled:

```
Array
(
    [key] => value
    [color] => 'red'
)
```

With magic_quotes_gpc enabled:

```
Array
(
    [key] => value
    [color] => \'red\'
)
```

See Also:

get_magic_quotes_gpc – Check if magic quotes is enabled
list() – Assign contents of an array to variables

♣ ♣ ♣

This is a handy way to easily convert all the query submitted keys/values from $_SERVER['QUERY_STRING'] into variables using the following:

```
parse_str($_SERVER['QUERY_STRING']);
```

str_replace(*find, replace, subject [, count]*)

find – **$string** or **$array**
replace – **$string** or **$array**
subject – **$string** or **$array**
count – [optional] **variable name - $integer**

Replaces all instances of *find* with *replace* within *subject*. If *subject* is an array, the *find* and *replace* occurs on all entries within the array.
If *find* and *replace* are arrays, the entire string is processed for each entry in the arrays, finding the first entry in *find* and replacing it with the first entry in *replace*, then repeating with the next set of entries. If there are more values in the *find* array than the *replace* array, an empty string ('') is used as the replacement. If *find* is an array and *replace* is a string, *replace* is used for every entry in *find*.
The optional *count* variable will be set with the total number of replacements that occurred.
***Note:** This function is case-sensitive.*

Examples:

```
$newstring = str_replace('find', 'replace', 'I will find');
echo $newstring;
```

```
I will replace
```

```
$array = array('I like dogs', 'I hate dogs');
$newarray = str_replace('dog', 'cat', $array);
print_r($newarray);
```

```
Array ( [0] => I like cats [1] => I hate cats )
```

```
$findarray = array('l', 'p');
$replacearray = array('p', 'x');
$string = "Hello";
// It will find l, replace with p, then find p and replace with x
$newstring = str_replace($findarray, $replacearray, $string, $count);
echo "$newstring had a total of $count replacements";
```

```
Hexxo had a total of 4 replacements
```

```
$findarray = array('l', 'p', 'x'); // has one extra entry
$replacearray = array('p', 'x');
$string = "Hello";
$newstring = str_replace($findarray, $replacearray, $string);
echo $newstring;
```

```
Heo
```

```
$findarray = array('l', 'o');
$replace = 'x';
$string = "Hello";
$newstring = str_replace($findarray, $replace, $string);
echo $newstring;
```

```
Hexxx
```

See Also:

str_ireplace() – Case-insensitive version of **str_replace()**
strtr() – Simplified variation that also does not repeat on *find/replace*

str_ireplace(*find, replace, subject [, count]*)

find – **$string** or **$array**
replace – **$string** or **$array**
subject – **$string** or **$array**
count – [optional] **variable name - $integer**

Replaces all instances of *find* with *replace* within *subject*. If subject is an array, the *find* and *replace* occurs on all entries within the array.
If find and replace are arrays, the entire string is processed for each entry in the arrays, finding the first entry in *find* and replacing it with the first entry in *replace*, then repeating with the next set of entries. If there are more values in the *find* array than the *replace* array, an empty string ('') is used as the replacement. If *find* is an array and *replace* is a string, *replace* is used for every entry in *find*.
The optional *count* variable will be set with the total number of replacements that occurred.
Note: *This function is case-insensitive.*

Example:

```
$newstring = str_ireplace('find', 'replace', 'I will FIND');
echo $newstring;
```

```
I will replace
```

See ***str_replace()*** *for more examples*

See Also:

str_replace() – Case-sensitive version of **str_ireplace()**

strtr($string, *find, replace*)
strtr($string, *replace_array*)

find – **$string**
replace – **$string**
replace_array – **$array**, associative *find* => *replace*

This function behaves differently if presented with either three arguments (single find/replace) or two arguments (uses an array of find/replace). With three arguments, all instances of *find* inside of **$string** are replaced with *replace*. With two arguments, each entry of *replace_array* is processed so that the key is replaced with the value.
Note: *Unlike* ***str_replace()****, only the original values of* ***$string*** *will be subject to the find/replace.*

Example:

```
echo strtr('I like dogs', 'dog', 'cat');
```

```
I like cats
```

```
$array = array( 'find' => 'replace', 'replace' => 'find');
$string = 'I will find and then replace';
$newstring = strtr($string, $array);
echo $newstring;
```

```
I will replace and then find
```

See Also:

str_replace() – A more flexible method of replacing items within a string

substr($string, *start [, length]*)

start – **$integer**, if negative, starts counting from the end of **$string**
length – [optional] **$integer** *default:* strlen(**$string**) if negative, number of characters left off from the end of **$string**

Returns only a portion of string starting with the character after number *start* and optionally for *length* characters long.

Examples:

```
echo substr('1234567890', 3);
```

```
4567890
```

```
echo substr('1234567890', -3, 1);
```

```
8
```

```
echo substr('1234567890', -3, -1);
```

```
89
```

substr_replace(*subject, replace, start [, length]*)

subject – **$string** or **$array**
replace – **$string**
start – **$integer**, if negative, counts from the end of the string
length – [optional] **$integer** *default:* strlen(**$string**)

Replaces text till the end of the string within *subject* with *replace* starting after character number *start*. If *length* is specified, only *length* number of characters after *start* are replaced with *replace* when *length* is positive. If *length* is negative, it represents the number of characters to stop replacing from the end of the string.
If *subject* is an array, the function returns an array instead of a string, with the replacement processed on every entry in the array.

Examples:

```
$string = substr_replace('1234567890', 'hello', 3);
echo $string;
```

```
123hello
```

```
echo substr_replace('1234567890', 'hello', 3, 2);
```

```
123hello67890
```

```
$array = array('1234567890', '0987654321');
$array = substr_replace($array, 'hello', -3, -2);
print_r($array);
```

```
Array ( [0] => 1234567hello90 [1] => 0987654hello21 )
```

See Also:

str_replace() – A find and replace of specific strings or array contents

substr_count(*haystack, needle* [*, start*] [*, length*])

haystack – **$string**
needle – **$string**
start – [optional] **$integer**, must be 0 or a positive number
length – [optional] **$integer**, must be 0 or a positive number

Returns the total number of instances of *needle* in *haystack*. If *start* is provided, it ignores *start* number of characters from the beginning. If *length* is provided, it only checks *length* characters from *start*.

Examples:

```
echo substr_count('abcdef', 'bc');
```

```
1
```

```
echo substr_count('abcdef', 'bc', 3);
```

```
0
```

str_pad($string, *pad_length* [, *pad_string*] [, *type*])

pad_length – **$integer**, must be positive and greater than strlen(**$string**)
pad_string – [optional] **$string** *default:* space (' ')
type – [optional] **$integer** (0, 1, or 2) *default:* 0 (pad right side only)
Other values: 1 (pad left side only)
2 (pad both sides)[12]

Inserts into **$string** spaces or the optional *pad_string* till **$string** is *pad_length* number of characters long.

Examples:

```
$string = 'Hello';
echo '<pre>'; // So preformatted text is shown
echo str_pad($string, 7), '|';
```

```
Hello  |
```

```
$string = 'Hello';
echo str_pad($string, 10, '#', 2);
```

```
##Hello###
```

See Also:

sprintf() – More complex function designed for formatting strings

str_repeat($string, *multiplier*)

multiplier – **$integer**

Returns a string with **$string** repeated *multiplier* times.

Example:

```
echo str_repeat('123', 3);
```

```
123123123
```

str_shuffle($string)

Randomly shuffles the characters in a string. A string jumble, essentially.

Example:

```
echo str_shuffle('Hello World!');
```

```
HreW! ollodl
```

12 Padding characters are alternated one-by-one, right side then left side

str_split($string *[, length]*)

length – [optional] **$integer**

Returns an array of **$string** separated by each character or the optional *length* number of characters.

Examples:

```
$array = str_split('Hello');
print_r($array);
```

```
Array ( [0] => H [1] => e [2] => l [3] => l [4] => o )
```

```
$array = str_split('Hello', 2);
print_r($array);
```

```
Array ( [0] => He [1] => ll [2] => o )
```

See Also:

chunk_split() – Splits a string after a specific length with \r\n and returns a string

str_word_count($string [*, option*] [*, characters*])

option – [optional] **$integer** (0, 1, or 2) *default:* 0 (returns: number of words)
Other values: 1 (returns: array containing all words found)
2 (returns: array with *position* => *word*)
characters – [optional] **$string**

Counts the number of words inside **$string** and returns that count by default (can be altered by *options*). If *characters* is present, it contains any characters that should be considered the same as a letter.

Examples:

```
$string = 'Welcome to the jungle';
echo str_word_count($string);
```

```
4
```

```
$string = 'Welcome to the jun3gle';
$without = str_word_count($string, 0);
$withchar = str_word_count($string, 0, '3');
echo "Without: $without, WithChar: $withchar";
```

```
Without: 5, WithChar: 4
```

```
$string = 'Welcome to the jungle';
echo '<pre>'; // For easier readability
$array = str_word_count($string, 1);
print_r($array);
```

```
Array
(
    [0] => Welcome
    [1] => to
    [2] => the
```

```
    [3] => jungle
)
```

```
$array = str_word_count($string, 2);
print_r($array);
```

```
Array
(
    [0] => Welcome
    [8] => to
    [11] => the
    [15] => jungle
)
```

strip_tags($string [, *allowed_tags*])

allowed_tags – [optional] **$string**

Remove HTML tags and comments from **$string**. If specific tags should be excluded, they can be specified inside *allowed_tags*.

Examples:

```
$string = "<p>This is a paragraph. </p><strong>Yay!</strong>";
echo strip_tags($string), strip_tags($string, '<p>');
```

HTML Source Code:

```
This is a paragraph. Yay!
```

```
echo strip_tags($string, '<p>');
```

```
<p>This is a paragraph. </p>Yay!
```

See Also:

htmlspecialchars() – Convert HTML special characters to their entity equivalent

strpos(*haystack, needle* [, *start*])

haystack – **$string**
needle – **$string**
start – [optional] **$integer**

Returns the position (number of characters from the beginning of *haystack*) of the first occurrence of *needle* in *haystack*. If *start* is included, searching begins after *start* number of characters.
Note: *If needle is not found in haystack, FALSE is returned. See tip below.*

Example:

```
$string = 'And now for something completely different';
$needle = 'thing';
echo strpos($string, $needle);
```

```
16
```

See Also:

strrpos() – Finds the last occurrence of *needle* in *haystack*
stripos() – Finds the first occurrence of *needle* in *haystack*, case insensitive

Note the following difference in evaluating the output of this function:

```
$string = 'hello';
$needle = 'h';
if (strpos($string,$needle) == FALSE){ // evaluating equality
    echo 'Not Found!';
}
```

```
Not Found!
```

Because strpos($string,$needle) equaled 0, and the boolean FALSE evaluates equal to the integer 0, the expression is true and the echo occurs. Therefore, it is important to evaluate the expression for an identical match (===).

```
$string = 'hello';
$needle = 'h';
if (strpos($string,$needle) === FALSE){ // identical evaluation
    echo 'Not Found!';
  }else{
    echo 'Found!';
}
```

```
Found!
```

strrpos(*haystack, needle* [, *start*])

haystack – **$string**
needle – **$string**
start – [optional] **$integer**

Returns the position (number of characters from the beginning of *haystack*) of the last occurrence of *needle* in *haystack*. If *start* is included and is a positive integer, searching begins after *start* number of characters; if negative, it stops searching *start* number of characters from the end of the string.
***Note:** If needle is not found in haystack, FALSE is returned. See **strpos()** for tip.*

Example:

```
$string = 'hello';
$needle = 'l';
echo strpos($string, $needle); // Search for first occurrence
echo '<br />'; // XHTML line break
echo strrpos($string, $needle); // Search for last occurrence
```

```
2
3
```

See Also:

strpos() – Finds the first occurrence of *needle* in *haystack*
strripos() – Finds the last occurrence of *needle* in *haystack*, case insensitive

stripos(*haystack, needle* [, *start*])

haystack – **$string**
needle – **$string**
start – [optional] **$integer**

Returns the position (number of characters from the beginning of *haystack*) of the first occurrence of *needle* in *haystack*, case insensitive. If *start* is included, searching begins after *start* number of characters.
Note: *If needle is not found in haystack, FALSE is returned. See* ***strpos()*** *for tip.*

Example:

```
$string = 'And now for something completely different';
$needle = 'NOW';
echo stripos($string, $needle);
```

```
4
```

See Also:

strripos() – Finds the last occurrence of *needle* in *haystack*, case insensitive
strpos() – Finds the first occurrence of *needle* in *haystack*, case sensitive

strripos(*haystack, needle* [, *start*])

haystack – **$string**
needle – **$string**
start – [optional] **$integer**

Returns the position (number of characters from the beginning of *haystack*) of the last occurrence of *needle* in *haystack*, case insensitive. If *start* is included and is a positive integer, searching begins after *start* number of characters; if negative, it stops searching *start* number of characters from the end of the string.
Note: *If needle is not found in haystack, FALSE is returned. See* ***strpos()*** *for tip.*

Example:

```
$string = 'hello';
$needle = 'L';
echo strrpos($string, $needle); // Search for last occurrence
```

```
3
```

See Also:

strrpos() – Finds the last occurrence of *needle* in *haystack*, case sensitive
stripos() – Finds the first occurrence of *needle* in *haystack*, case insensitive

strstr(*haystack, needle*)

haystack – **$string**
needle – **$string**

Find if *needle* is found in *haystack* and returns the first occurrence of *needle* to the end of *haystack*.
Note: *If needle is not found in haystack, FALSE is returned.*

Example:

```
$string = 'www.example.com';
$needle = 'example';
echo strstr($string, $needle);
```

```
example.com
```

See Also:

stristr() – case insensitive version of **strstr()**

stristr(*haystack, needle*)

haystack – **$string**
needle – **$string**

Finds if *needle* is found in *haystack* and returns the first occurrence of *needle* to the end of *haystack*, case insensitive.
Note: *If needle is not found in haystack, FALSE is returned.*

Example:

```
$string = 'www.example.com';
$needle = 'EXAMPLE';
echo stristr($string, $needle);
```

```
example.com
```

See Also:

strstr() – case sensitive version of **stristr()**

strlen($string)

The length of **$string**, or 0 if it is empty.

Example:

```
$string = 'Hello!';
echo strlen($string);
```

```
6
```

strtolower($string)

Converts all characters in **$string** to lowercase and returns the new string.

Example:

```
$string = 'Mario Lurig';
echo strtolower($string);
```

```
mario lurig
```

strtoupper($string)

Converts all characters in **$string** to uppercase and returns the new string.

Example:

```
$string = 'Mario Lurig';
echo strtoupper($string);
```

```
MARIO LURIG
```

ucfirst($string)

Converts the first character in **$string** to uppercase and returns the new string.

Example:

```
$string = 'i wish i had some capitalization';
echo ucfirst($string);
```

```
I wish i had some capitalization
```

ucwords($string)

Converts the first alphabetic characters of words in **$string** to uppercase and returns the new string.

Example:

```
$string = 'i wish i had 3three some capitalization';
echo ucwords($string);
```

```
I Wish I Had 3three Some Capitalization
```

strpbrk(*haystack, characters*)

haystack – **$string**
characters – **$string**

Find if any of the characters in *needle* are found in *haystack* and returns the first occurrence of the character found in *needle* to the end of *haystack*.
Note: *If needle is not found in haystack, FALSE is returned.*

Example:

```
$string = 'www.example.com/index.htm';
$needle = './c';
echo strpbrk($string, $needle); // Finds the period (.) first
```

```
.example.com/index.htm
```

See Also:

strstr() – Same as **strpbrk()** but searches for a string instead of characters

strrev($string)

Reverses a string.

Example:

```
echo strrev('hello world');
```

```
dlrow olleh
```

Array Functions

It took me a while to learn about arrays, they were these scary things with keys and values, associative and indexed, and then you could have an array inside an array... I was scared. Truth was, they were infinitely useful in keeping things organized, efficient, and quick. Without **foreach**, code would be bloated 2-3 times what it could be. So don't be scared, and learn to love arrays.

One quick note: For easier readability, the output in this section is surrounded by the HTML <pre> (preformatted) tag for easier readability if an array contains more than one entry. Unlike all other chapters where it is included in the supplied code, it is not in this chapter as a space consideration.

Array Nomenclature

Common usage and syntax for arrays.

Example:

```
$array = array(); // Define $array as... an array
$array = array( 'value', 'two', 'three' ); // Indexed array
$array = array( 'key' => 'value', 'job' => 'slacker' ); // Associative

$array = array();
$array[] = 'value'; // Assign value to next available indexed key
$array[0] = 'value'; // Assign value to the key of 0
$array['name'] = 'value'; // Assign value to the key name

// Assign the value of key 0 in $array to $value
$value = $array[0];

// Assign the value of the key name in $array to $value
$value = $array['name'];
```

array_change_key_case($array [, *option*])

option – [optional] **$integer** (0 or 1) *default:* 0 (lowercase)
Other value: 1 (uppercase)

Changes the case of the keys inside of **$array** to lowercase (*default*) or uppercase.

Examples:

```
$array = array( 'NaMe' => 'BoB' );
print_r( array_change_key_case($array) );
```

```
Array ( [name] => BoB )
```

```
print_r( array_change_key_case($array, 1) );
```

```
Array ( [NAME] => BoB )
```

array_chunk($array, *size* [, *preserve_keys*])

size – **$integer**
preserve_keys – [optional] **$boolean** *default:* FALSE, array is reindexed numerically

Splits the **$array** by the *size* number of values for each new array, returning a multi-dimensional indexed array. If *preserve_keys* is not specified, the values are reindexed in an indexed array. If *preserve_keys* is set to TRUE, keys are retained.

Example:

```
$array = array( 'name' => 'bob', 'job' => 'dad' );
$newarray = array_chunk($array, 1);
print_r($newarray);
```

```
Array
(
    [0] => Array
        (
            [0] => bob
        )
    [1] => Array
        (
            [0] => dad
        )
)
```

```
$array = array( 'name' => 'bob', 'job' => 'dad' );
$newarray = array_chunk($array, 1, TRUE);
print_r($newarray);
```

```
Array
(
    [0] => Array
        (
            [name] => bob
        )
```

```
    [1] => Array
        (
            [job] => dad
        )
)
```

array_combine(*key_array, value_array*)

key_array – **$array**
value_array – **$array**

Creates a new array using the values from *key_array* as the keys and the values from *value_array* as the values.
Note: *Returns FALSE if number of entries in both arrays does not match.*

Example:

```
$keys = array ( 'name', 'job', 'age' );
$values = array ( 'Bob', 'knight', 42 );
$newarray = array_combine($keys, $values);
print_r($newarray);
```

```
Array
(
    [name] => Bob
    [job] => knight
    [age] => 42
)
```

See Also:

array_merge() – Combine the keys and values of multiple arrays

array_merge($array [, ...$array...])

Can accept multiple array values, and behaves differently with only one argument

If supplied with only one indexed **$array**, it reindexes that array continuously.
If supplied with more than one **$array**, the content of both arrays are combined with all indexed keys included in the new array, while associative keys that are identical take the value of the last **$array** supplied.

Example:

```
$array = array ( 3 => 'one', 0 => 'two', 2 => 'three' );
print_r( array_merge($array) );
```

```
Array
(
    [0] => one
    [1] => two
    [2] => three
)
```

```
$array = array ( 'zero', 'one', 'name' => 'Bob' );
$array2 = array ( 'alsozero', 'name' => 'John', 'job' => 'farmer' );
print_r( array_merge($array, $array2) );
```

```
Array
(
    [0] => zero
    [1] => one
    [name] => John
    [2] => alsozero
    [job] => farmer
)
```

See Also:

array_combine() – Combine the values of two arrays into a key=>value array

If you want to combine two arrays and do not mind if values with the same keys accept the values from the first array and discard any other arrays supplied, simply use the plus sign (+).

```
$array = array ( 'zero', 'name' => 'Bob', 'job' => 'player' );
$array2 = array ( 'alsozero', 'job' => 'farmer' );
print_r( $array + $array2 );
```

```
Array
(
    [0] => zero
    [name] => Bob
    [job] => player
)
```

array_count_values($array)

Returns an array with the unique values in **$array** as the keys and their count as the values.

Note: *Does not work for multi-dimensional arrays.*

Example:

```
$array = array ( 'zero', 'one', 'zero' );
print_r( array_count_values($array) );
```

```
Array
(
    [zero] => 2
    [one] => 1
)
```

See Also:

count() – Count the total number of entries in an array

count($array [, *mode*])

mode – [optional] **$integer** *default:* 0, does not count multidimensional arrays
Other value: 1, counts entries within multidimensional arrays

Counts the number of elements in **$array**. By default, entries within arrays that are part of **$array** (multidimensional arrays) are not counted unless *mode* is set to 1.

Examples:

```
$array = array ('zero',
                'names' => array ( 'john', 'dave' ),
                'ages' => array ( 22, 34 )          );
echo count($array);
```

```
3
```

```
echo count($array, 1);
```

```
7
```

See Also:

array_count_values() – Get the number of unique values inside of an array

array_diff(*first_array*, $array [, ...$array...])

Accepts multiple $array for comparison against first_array
first_array – **$array**

Compares the values of all **$array**(s) against the values in *first_array* and returns an array with the entries of *first_array* which do not share values with entries in **$array**(s).

Example:

```
$array = array( 'one', 'two', 'three', 'four' );
$array2 = array( 'two', 'three' );
$array3 = array( 'bob' => 'one' );
 // value is 'one', matching $array
print_r( array_diff($array, $array2, $array3) );
```

```
Array ( [3] => four )
```

See Also:

array_diff_key() – Same comparison, but based on keys instead of values
array_diff_assoc() – Same comparison, but based on both keys and values
array_intersect() – Similar, but returns entries that are present in all **$array**(s)

array_diff_key(*first_array*, $array [, ...$array...])

*Accepts multiple **$array** for comparison against first_array*
first_array – **$array**

Compares the keys of all **$array**(s) against the keys in *first_array* and returns an array with the entries of *first_array* which do not share keys with entries in **$array**(s).

Example:

```
$array = array( 'zero', 'name' => 'john', 'job' => 'john' );
$array2 = array( 'alsozero', 'job' => 'john' );
print_r( array_diff_key($array, $array2));
```

```
Array ( [name] => john )
```

See Also:

array_diff() – Same comparison, but based on values only
array_diff_assoc() – Same comparison, but based on both keys and values

array_diff_assoc(*first_array*, $array [, ...$array...])

*Accepts multiple **$array** for comparison against first_array*
first_array – **$array**

Compares the contents of all **$array**(s) against the keys and values in *first_array* and returns an array with the entries of *first_array* which do not share exact keys and values with entries in **$array**(s).

Example:

```
$array = array( 'zero', 'one', 'name' => 'john' );
$array2 = array( 'zero', 'alsoone', 'name' => 'john' );
print_r( array_diff_assoc($array, $array2) );
```

```
Array ( [1] => one )
```

See Also:

array_diff_key() – Same comparison, but based on keys instead of values
array_diff() – Same comparison, but based on values only

array_intersect(*first_array*, $array [, ...$array...])

*Accepts multiple **$array** for comparison against first_array*
first_array – **$array**

Compares the values of all **$array**(s) against the values in *first_array* and returns an array with the entries of *first_array* which share values with entries from <u>all</u> **$array**(s).

Example:

```
$array = array( 'one', 'two');
$array2 = array( 'two', 'one', 'three', 'four' ); // 'one','two' match
$array3 = array( 'bob' => 'one' );

 // only 'one' matches
print_r( array_intersect($array, $array2, $array3) );
```

```
Array ( [0] => one )
```

See Also:

array_intersect_key() – Same comparison, but based on keys
array_intersect_assoc() – Same comparison, but based on both keys and values
array_diff() – Similar, but returns entries that are not present in **$array**(s)

array_intersect_key(*first_array*, $array [, ...$array...])

*Accepts multiple **$array** for comparison against first_array*
first_array – **$array**

Compares the keys of all **$array**(s) against the keys in *first_array* and returns an array with the entries of *first_array* which share keys with entries from all **$array**(s).

Example:

```
$array = array( 'zero', 'name' => 'john', 'job' => 'john' );
$array2 = array( 'alsozero', 'job' => 'john' );
print_r( array_intersect_key($array, $array2));
```

```
Array
(
    [0] => zero
    [job] => john
)
```

See Also:

array_intersect() – Same comparison, but based on values only
array_intersect_assoc() – Same comparison, but based on both keys and values

array_intersect_assoc(*first_array*, $array [, ...$array...])

Accepts multiple $array for comparison against first_array
first_array – **$array**

Compares the contents of all **$array**(s) against the keys and values in *first_array* and returns an array with the entries of *first_array* which share exact keys and values with entries from all **$array**(s).

Example:

```
$array = array( 'zero', 'one', 'name' => 'john' );
$array2 = array( 'zero', 'alsoone', 'name' => 'john' );
print_r( array_intersect_assoc($array, $array2) );
```

```
Array
(
    [0] => zero
    [name] => john
)
```

See Also:

array_intersect_key() – Same comparison, but based on keys
array_intersect() – Same comparison, but based on values only

array_flip($array)

Returns an array with they keys of **$array** as values, and the values of **$array** as the new keys. Be aware that if the original value is not a **$string** or **$integer** and it will not be converted and an error will be generated (See tip below).
Note: *Any original values that are the same as previous original values, when flipped to be a key, will overwrite the previous original value/key.*

Example:

```
$array = array( 'CEO' => 'Bob', 'zero', 'Owner' => 'Bob' );
print_r( array_flip($array) );
```

```
Array
(
    [Bob] => Owner
    [zero] => 0
)
```

See Also:

array_reverse() – Reverses the order of entire entities in an array

If there is no concern for **$boolean** or **$float** values being removed after the flip, you can suppress errors (@) on **array_flip()** so that they are ignored.

```
$array = array( 'CEO' => 'Bob', 'good guy' => TRUE );
$newarray = @array_flip($array);
print_r($newarray);
```

```
Array ( [Bob] => CEO )
```

array_reverse($array [, *preserve_keys*])

preserve_keys – [optional] **$boolean** *default:* FALSE, indexed keys are reindexed

Returns an array which contains the **$array** in reverse order, with indexed keys destroyed and reindexed by default. If *preserve_keys* is set to TRUE, the original keys will be kept.

Example:

```
$array = array( 'zero',
                'one',
                'two',
                array( 'zero', 'name' => 'Bob' ) );
print_r( array_reverse($array) );
```

```
Array
(
    [0] => Array
        (
            [0] => zero
            [name] => Bob
        )
    [1] => two
    [2] => one
    [3] => zero
)
```

```
print_r( array_reverse($array, TRUE) );
```

```
Array
(
    [3] => Array
        (
            [0] => zero
            [name] => Bob
        )
    [2] => two
    [1] => one
    [0] => zero
)
```

See Also:

array_flip() – Switch the keys and values within an array

array_key_exists(*key*, $array)

key – **$string** or **$integer**

Returns TRUE if *key* is present within **$array**.

Example:

```
$array = array( 'name' => 'John', 'job' => 'unknown' );
var_dump( array_key_exists('name', $array) );
```

```
bool(true)
```

See Also:

array_search() – Similar, except returns the key if it is found
in_array() – Checks whether a specific value exists in an array

array_search(*search_value*, $array [, *strict*])

search_value – **$variable**
strict – [optional] **$boolean** *default:* FALSE, match value only, not type of variable

Checks whether *search_value*[13] exists in **$array** and returns its key if present. If it is not found, FALSE is returned. If *strict* is set to TRUE, **array_search()** will only return TRUE if the value and its variable type matches as well.
Note: *Only the first instance of search_value found returns its key. If the same value is present later in the array, it is ignored.*

Example:

```
$array = array( 'name' => 'Bob', 'age' => 12, 'title' => 'owner' );
echo array_search('owner', $array);
```

```
title
```

```
$array = array( 'name' => 'Bob', 'age' => 12, 'title' => 'owner' );
var_dump( array_search('12', $array, TRUE) );
// Because strict is TRUE, string '12' does not match integer 12
```

```
bool(false)
```

See Also:

array_keys() – Similar, except it returns multiple keys with the same value
array_key_exists() – Similar, except returns only TRUE or FALSE
in_array() – Checks whether a specific value exists in an array

in_array(*value*, $array [, *strict*])

value –**$variable**
strict – [optional] **$boolean** *default:* FALSE, match value only, not type of variable

Returns TRUE if *value* is present within **$array**. If *strict* is set to TRUE, **in_array()** will only return TRUE if the *value* and the variable type matches as well.

13 If *search_value* is a string, it is evaluated as case-sensitive

Example:

```
$array = array( 'name' => 'John', 'age' => '12' ); // '12' is a string
$integer = 12; // 12 is an integer
var_dump( in_array( $integer, $array) );
```

```
bool(true)
```

```
var_dump( in_array( $integer, $array, TRUE) );
```

```
bool(false)
```

See Also:

array_key_exists() – Checks whether a specific key exists in an array
array_search() – Checks whether a specific key exists and returns it

array_keys($array [, *search_value*] [, *strict*])

search_value – [optional] **$variable**
strict – [optional] **$boolean** *default:* FALSE, match value only, not type of variable

Returns an array with all the keys in **$array**. If *search_value* is present, it only returns the keys that contain *search_value*. If *strict* is set to TRUE, *search_value* will be considered a match if the value and the type of variable are correct.

Example:

```
$array = array( 'name' => 'Bob', 'nickname' => 'Bob', 'age' => '12' );
print_r( array_keys($array) );
```

```
Array
(
    [0] => name
    [1] => nickname
    [2] => age
)
```

```
$array = array( 'name' => 'Bob', 'nickname' => 'Bob', 'age' => '12' );
print_r( array_keys($array, 'Bob') );
```

```
Array
(
    [0] => name
    [1] => nickname
)
```

```
// Notice that the 12 key is a string, not the indexed value of 12
$array = array( 'name' => 'Bob', 'nickname' => 'Bob', '12' => 'age' );
$integer = 12;
print_r( array_keys($array, $integer, TRUE) );
```

```
Array ( )
```

See Also:

array_values() – Returns all the values in an array

array_values($array)

Return all the values in **$array** as an indexed array.

Example:

```
$array = array( 'name' => 'Eric', 'age' => 12, 'zero' );
print_r( array_values($array) );
```

```
Array
(
    [0] => Eric
    [1] => 12
    [2] => zero
)
```

See Also:

array_keys() – Returns all the keys in an array (or keys matching a specific value)

array_multisort($array [, *order*] [, *type*] [, ...$array [, *order*] [, *type*]...])

Can accept multiple $array with their own optional order and type flags
order – [optional] *default:* SORT_ASC (ascending)
Other value: SORT_DESC (descending)
type – [optional] *default:* SORT_REGULAR (compare items normally)
Other values: SORT_NUMERIC (compare items numerically)
SORT_STRING (compare items as strings)

Sorts the **$array** ascending by their values unless altered by the *order* and *type* flags. All indexed (numeric) keys will be rewritten, while associative keys will be unchanged. Sorting of uppercase letters is prior to lowercase letters when sorting in ascending order. Be aware that this function effects **$array** directly, and returns TRUE on success.
Note: *If multiple $array are provided, unless order and type flags are included, each array uses the default order and type flags are set (SORT_ASC, SORT_REGULAR).*

Example:

```
$array = array( '2', '3', '1', 'a', 'b');
array_multisort($array);
print_r($array);
```

```
Array
(
    [0] => 1
    [1] => 2
    [2] => 3
    [3] => a
    [4] => b
)
```

```
$array = array( '2', '3', '1', 'a', 'b');
array_multisort($array, SORT_NUMERIC);
print_r($array);
```

```
Array
(
    [0] => b
    [1] => a
    [2] => 1
    [3] => 2
    [4] => 3
)
```

```
$array = array( '2', '3', '1', 'a', 'b');
array_multisort($array, SORT_DESC, SORT_NUMERIC);
print_r($array);
```

```
Array
(
    [0] => 3
    [1] => 2
    [2] => 1
    [3] => b
    [4] => a
)
```

```
$array = array( '2', '3', '1', 'a', 'b');
array_multisort($array, SORT_DESC, SORT_STRING);
print_r($array);
```

```
Array
(
    [0] => b
    [1] => a
    [2] => 3
    [3] => 2
    [4] => 1
)
```

♣ ♣ ♣

This function is similar to the ORDER BY option of MySQL queries.

array_pop($array)

Returns the last value in **$array** and removes it from the array.

Example:

```
$array = array('zero', 'one', 'two');
$value = array_pop($array);
echo $value;
```

```
two
```

```
print_r($array);
```

```
Array
(
 [0] => zero
 [1] => one
)
```

See Also:

array_shift() – Similar to array_pop, but to the beginning of the array
array_unshift() – Adds values onto the beginning of an array
array_push() – Adds values onto the end of an array
array_splice() – Similar, but is flexible enough to do other things as well

array_push($array, *value* [, ...*value*...])

Can accept multiple values
value – **$variable**

Adds *value*(s) to **$array**, equivalent to:

```
$array[] = value;
```

The above is the preferred method if adding a single *value*.

Example:

```
$array = array('zero');
array_push($array, 'one', 'two');
print_r($array);
```

```
Array
(
    [0] => zero
    [1] => one
    [2] => two
)
```

See Also:

array_unshift() – Adds values onto the beginning of an array
array_pop() – Removes the last value from the end of an array
array_shift() – Similar to array_pop, but to the beginning of the array
array_splice() – Similar, but is flexible enough to do other things as well

array_shift($array)

Returns the first value in **$array** and removes it from the array, reindexing all numerical keys.

Example:

```
$array = array('zero', 'one', 'two', 'name' => 'Bob');
$value = array_shift($array);
echo $value;
```

```
zero
```

```
print_r($array);
```

```
Array
(
    [0] => one
    [1] => two
    [name] => Bob
)
```

See Also:

array_unshift() – Adds values onto the beginning of an array
array_pop() – Removes the last value from the end of an array
array_push() – Adds values onto the end of an array
array_splice() – Similar, but is flexible enough to do other things as well

array_unshift($array, *value* [, *...value...*])

Can accept multiple values
value – **$variable**

Adds *value*(s) to the beginning of **$array**, reindexing all numerical keys.

Example:

```
$array = array('zero');
array_unshift($array, 'one', 'two');
print_r($array);
```

```
Array
(
    [0] => one
    [1] => two
    [2] => zero
)
```

See Also:

array_push() – Adds values onto the end of an array
array_pop() – Removes the last value from the end of an array
array_shift() – Similar to array_pop, but to the beginning of the array
array_splice() – Similar, but is flexible enough to do other things as well

array_product($array)

Returns the product (multiplication) of values in **$array**.
Note: *If any values in the array cannot be evaluated as an integer,* ***array_product()*** *returns the integer 0.*

Examples:

```
$array = array( 2, 4, 8 );
echo array_product($array);
```

```
64
```

```
$array = array( '2', '4', '8' );
var_dump( array_product($array) );
```

```
int(64)
```

array_sum($array)

Returns the sum (addition) of values in **$array**.

Note: *Any values in the array that cannot be evaluated as an integer are ignored.*

Examples:

```
$array = array( 2, 4, 8 );
echo array_sum($array);
```

```
14
```

```
$array = array( '2', '4', '8', 'blah' );
var_dump( array_sum($array) );
```

```
int(14)
```

array_rand($array [, *count*])

count – [optional] **$integer** *default:* 1

Returns a string containing a randomly selected key from **$array**. If *count* is supplied and greater than 1, it specifies the number of keys to select randomly from **$array** and returns an array.

Examples:

```
$array = array( 'name' => 'Bob', 'job' => 'n/a', 'age' => 12 );
$random_key = array_rand($array);
echo $random_key; // Results will vary
```

```
job
```

```
$array = array( 'name' => 'Bob', 'job' => 'n/a', 'age' => 12 );
$random_array = array_rand($array, 2);
print_r($random_array); // Results will vary
```

```
Array
(
    [0] => age
    [1] => name
)
```

See Also:

shuffle() – Randomizes the values in an array

This function is meant to be combined with other code, since it only retrieves the key(s). Here is a simple usage example on an indexed array containing keywords, possibly retrieved from a database.

```
$array = array( 'css', 'php', 'xml', 'html', 'xhtml', 'tutorial' );
$rand_key = array_rand($array);
$keyword = $array[$rand_key];
echo $keyword; // Results will vary
```

```
html
```

shuffle($array)

Randomizes the values in **$array**, returning TRUE if successful.
Note: *All keys, including associative, are removed and the entire array is reindexed.*

Example:

```
$array = array( 'zero' => 'zero', 'one' => 'one', 'two' => 'two');
shuffle($array); // Results will vary
print_r($array);
```

```
Array
(
    [0] => one
    [1] => zero
    [2] => two
)
```

See Also:

array_rand() – Returns one or more random keys from an array

array_slice($array, *offset* [, *length*] [, *preserve_keys*])

offset – **$integer**
length – [optional] **$integer** *default:* till end of **$array**
preserve_keys – [optional] **$boolean** *default:* FALSE, indexed keys are reindexed

Selects the entries in **$array** from the *offset* where a positive *offset* will skip *offset* number of entries from the beginning, while a negative *offset* will start from *offset* number of entries from the end.
If *length* is specified and positive, it determines the maximum number of entries returned from *offset*. If *length* is negative, it specifies stopping that many entries from the end of **$array** after *offset*.
By default, any indexed keys will be reindexed in the returned array of results. If *preserve_keys* is set to TRUE, the original keys will be represented in the result array.

Example:

```
$array = array( 'zero', 'one', 'two', 'three', 'four', 'five' );
$result_array = array_slice($array, 3);
print_r($result_array);
```

```
Array
(
    [0] => three
    [1] => four
    [2] => five
)
```

```
$array = array( 'zero', 'one', 'two', 'three', 'four', 'five' );
$result_array = array_slice($array, 3, 1);
print_r($result_array);
```

```
Array ( [0] => three )
```

```
$array = array( 'zero', 'one', 'two', 'three', 'four', 'five' );
$result_array = array_slice($array, -4, -1, TRUE);
print_r($result_array);
```

```
Array
(
    [2] => two
    [3] => three
    [4] => four
)
```

array_splice($array, *offset* [, *length*] [, *replacement*])

offset – **$integer**
length – [optional] **$integer** *default:* till end of **$array**
replacement – [optional] **$variable**

Alters **$array** based on the *offset* and other optional arguments, returning any removed entries in an array and replacing them with the optional *replacement*.
If *offset* is positive, the function will skip *offset* number of entries in **$array**[14]. If *offset* is negative, it will start *offset* number of entries from the end.
If *length* is specified and positive, it determines the maximum number of entries returned from *offset*. If *length* is negative, it specifies stopping that many entries from the end of **$array** after *offset*. If *length* is 0, nothing is removed.
When *replacement* is specified, removed entries from **$array** are replaced with *replacement*. If nothing was removed, the contents of *replacement* are inserted into **$array** based on the *offset*.
Note: *Indexed keys in **$array** may be reindexed.*

14 Use count($array) to specify the end of the array in *offset*

Examples:

```
$array = array( 'zero', 'one', 'two' );
$result_array = array_splice($array, 1);
print_r($array);
```

```
Array ( [0] => zero )
```

```
print_r($result_array);
```

```
Array
(
    [0] => one
    [1] => two
)
```

```
$array = array( 'zero', 'one', 'two' );
$result_array = array_splice($array, -2, 1);
print_r($array);
```

```
Array
(
    [0] => zero
    [1] => two
)
```

```
print_r($result_array);
```

```
Array ( [0] => one )
```

```
$array = array( 'zero', 'one' );
array_splice($array, count($array), 0, 'end');
print_r($array);
```

```
Array
(
    [0] => zero
    [1] => one
    [2] => end
)
```

```
$array = array( 'zero', 'one', 'two' );
array_splice($array, 2, 0, 'middle');
print_r($array);
```

```
Array
(
    [0] => zero
    [1] => one
    [2] => middle
    [3] => two
)
```

```
$array = array( 'zero', 'one', 'two' );
$result_array = array_splice($array, 1, 1, 'middle');
print_r($result_array);
```

```
Array ( [0] => one )
```

```
print_r($array);
```

```
Array
(
    [0] => zero
    [1] => middle
    [2] => two
)
```

```
$array = array( 0, 1 );
$replace_array = array( 'zero', 'one' );
array_splice($array, 0, 0, $replace_array);
print_r($array);
```

```
Array
(
    [0] => zero
    [1] => one
    [2] => 0
    [3] => 1
)
```

See Also:

array_shift($array**)** – `array_splice($array, 0, 1)`

array_unshift($array,*input***)** – `array_splice($array, 0, 0, input)`

array_push($array,*input***)** – `array_splice($array, count($array), 0, input)`

array_pop($array**)** – `array_splice($array, -1)`

array_unique($array)

Returns an array with all entries in **$array** with duplicate values removed.

Example:

```
$array = array( 'zero', 'one', 'zero', 'three' );
$newarray = array_unique($array);
print_r($newarray);
```

```
Array
(
    [0] => zero
    [1] => one
    [3] => three
)
```

sort($array [, *sort_flag*])

sort_flag – [optional] *default:* SORT_REGULAR (compare items normally)
Other values: SORT_NUMERIC (compare items numerically)
SORT_STRING (compare items as strings)
SORT_LOCALE_STRING (based on locale)

Sorts **$array** values from lowest to highest and reindexes all values, destroying all keys. By default, items are compared normally, but this can be altered based upon the inclusion of *sort_flag* options.

Examples:

```
$array = array( 'babe', 1, 'name' => 'Bob' );
sort($array);
print_r($array);
```

```
Array
(
    [0] => Bob
    [1] => babe
    [2] => 1
)
```

```
$array = array( 'babe', 1, 'name' => 'Bob' );
sort($array, SORT_NUMERIC);
print_r($array);
```

```
Array
(
    [0] => babe
    [1] => Bob
    [2] => 1
)
```

```
$array = array( 'babe', 1, 'name' => 'Bob' );
sort($array, SORT_STRING);
print_r($array);
```

```
Array
(
    [0] => 1
    [1] => Bob
    [2] => babe
)
```

See Also:

rsort() – Similar, except in reverse
asort() – Similar, except keys are maintained
ksort() – Similar, except keys are sorted instead of values
array_multisort() - Works on multiple arrays and is more flexible

rsort($array [, *sort_flag*])

sort_flag – [optional] *default:* SORT_REGULAR (compare items normally)
Other values: SORT_NUMERIC (compare items numerically)
SORT_STRING (compare items as strings)
SORT_LOCALE_STRING (based on locale)

Sorts **$array** values from highest to lowest and reindexes all values, destroying all keys. By default, items are compared normally, but this can be altered based upon the inclusion of *sort_flag* options.

Example:

```
$array = array( 'babe', 'apple', 'name' => 'Bob' );
rsort($array);
print_r($array);
```

```
Array
(
    [0] => babe
    [1] => apple
    [2] => Bob
)
```

See Also:

sort() – Similar, except from lowest to highest (also has more *sort_flag* examples)
arsort() – Similar, except keys are maintained
krsort() – Similar, except keys are sorted instead of values
array_multisort() - Works on multiple arrays and is more flexible

asort($array [, *sort_flag*])

sort_flag – [optional] *default:* SORT_REGULAR (compare items normally)
Other values: SORT_NUMERIC (compare items numerically)
SORT_STRING (compare items as strings)
SORT_LOCALE_STRING (based on locale)

Sorts **$array** values from lowest to highest maintaining keys. By default, items are compared normally, but this can be altered based upon the inclusion of *sort_flag* options.

Example:

```
$array = array( 'babe', 'apple', 'name' => 'Bob' );
asort($array);
print_r($array);
```

```
Array
(
    [name] => Bob
    [1] => apple
    [0] => babe
)
```

See Also:

sort() – Similar, except keys are destroyed (also has more *sort_flag* examples)
arsort() – Similar, except in reverse
ksort() – Similar, except keys are sorted instead of values
array_multisort() - Works on multiple arrays and is more flexible

arsort($array [, *sort_flag*])

sort_flag – [optional] *default:* SORT_REGULAR (compare items normally)
Other values: SORT_NUMERIC (compare items numerically)
SORT_STRING (compare items as strings)
SORT_LOCALE_STRING (based on locale)

Sorts **$array** values from highest to lowest maintaining keys. By default, items are compared normally, but this can be altered based upon the inclusion of *sort_flag* options.

Example:

```
$array = array( 'babe', 'apple', 'name' => 'Bob' );
arsort($array);
print_r($array);
```

```
Array
(
    [0] => babe
    [1] => apple
    [name] => Bob
)
```

See Also:

sort() – Similar, except from lowest to highest and keys are destroyed (also has more *sort_flag* examples)
asort() – Similar, except from lowest to highest
krsort() – Similar, except keys are sorted instead of values
array_multisort() - Works on multiple arrays and is more flexible

ksort($array [, *sort_flag*])

sort_flag – [optional] *default:* SORT_REGULAR (compare items normally)
Other values: SORT_NUMERIC (compare items numerically)
SORT_STRING (compare items as strings)
SORT_LOCALE_STRING (based on locale)

Sorts **$array** entries from lowest to highest by their keys. By default, items are compared normally, but this can be altered based upon the inclusion of *sort_flag* options.

Example:

```
$array = array( 'cute', 'fruit' => 'apple', 'name' => 'Bob' );
ksort($array);
print_r($array);
```

```
Array
(
    [0] => cute
    [fruit] => apple
    [name] => Bob
)
```

See Also:

sort() – Similar, except values are sorted instead of keys and keys are destroyed (also has more *sort_flag* examples)
krsort() – Similar, except in reverse
asort() – Similar, except values are sorted instead of keys
array_multisort() - Works on multiple arrays and is more flexible

krsort($array [, *sort_flag*])

sort_flag – [optional] *default:* SORT_REGULAR (compare items normally)
Other values: SORT_NUMERIC (compare items numerically)
SORT_STRING (compare items as strings)
SORT_LOCALE_STRING (based on locale)

Sorts **$array** entries from highest to lowest by their keys. By default, items are compared normally, but this can be altered based upon the inclusion of *sort_flag* options.

Example:

```
$array = array( 'cute', 'fruit' => 'apple', 'name' => 'Bob' );
krsort($array);
print_r($array);
```

```
Array
(
    [name] => Bob
    [fruit] => apple
    [0] => cute
)
```

See Also:

sort() – Similar, except from lowest to highest, values are sorted instead of keys, and keys are destroyed (also has more *sort_flag* examples)
ksort() – Similar, except from lowest to highest
arsort() – Similar, except values are sorted instead of keys
array_multisort() - Works on multiple arrays and is more flexible

compact(*variable_name* [, *...variable_name...*])

Can accept multiple variable_names
variable_name – **$string** or **$array**

Creates an array containing entries composed of a key equal to *variable_name* and value equal to the value of *variable_name*. If *variable_name* is an array, then values of that array are used as the variable names.
Note: *Global variables cannot be used with **compact()**.*

Example:

```
$variable = 'value';
$integer = 10;
$name = 'Bob';
$age = 12;
$array = array( 'name', 'age' ); // Names of variables as values
$result_array = compact('variable', 'integer', $array);
print_r($result_array);
```

```
Array
(
    [variable] => value
    [integer] => 10
    [name] => Bob
    [age] => 12
)
```

See Also:

extract() – Takes an array and assigns its keys as variables with their values

extract($array [, *type* [, *prefix*]])

type – [optional] *default:* EXTR_OVERWRITE (if collision, overwrite)
Other values: EXTR_SKIP (if collision, skip, don't overwrite)
EXTR_PREFIX_SAME (if collision, prefix with *prefix*)
EXTR_PREFIX_ALL (prefix all with *prefix*)
EXTR_PREFIX_INVALID (prefix invalid/numeric w/ *prefix*)
EXTR_IF_EXISTS (only overwrite variables that exist, else skip)
EXTR_PREFIX_IF_EXISTS (if variable already exists, create with prefix of *prefix*, else skip)
EXTR_REFS (extract variables as references)
prefix – [optional] only required with *type*s with _PREFIX_ in their value

Takes the entries in **$array** and assigns them to variables using the keys as the variable names and the array values as the variable's value. Returns the number of successfully written variables. The default behavior is to overwrite any variables that already exist, but this can be altered with *type*.

The *prefix* option is required if *type* is set to a value that includes _PREFIX_ in its name. If that *type* is set, the value of *prefix* must be used[15].
Note: *Be careful when applying* ***extract()*** *to user submitted data ($_REQUEST). Consider using the EXTR_IF_EXISTS type and defining the variables with empty values prior to running* ***extract()****.*

Examples:

```
$name = 'John';
$array = array( 'name' => 'Bob', 'age' => 32 );
$number_of_variables_created = extract($array);
echo "$name - $age";
```

```
Bob - 32
```

```
$name = 'John';
$array = array( 'name' => 'Bob', 'age' => 32 );
$number_variables_created = extract($array, EXTR_SKIP);
echo "$name - $age";
```

```
John - 32
```

```
$name = 'John';
$array = array( 'name' => 'Bob', 'age' => 32 );
$number_of_variables = extract($array, EXTR_PREFIX_SAME, 'prefix');
echo "$name - $age, $prefix_name - $age";
```

```
John - 32, Bob - 32
```

```
$name = 'John';
$array = array( 'name' => 'Bob', 'age' => 32 );
$number_of_variables = extract($array, EXTR_PREFIX_ALL, 'add');
echo "$name, $add_name - $add_age";
```

```
John, Bob - 32
```

See Also:

compact() – Takes variables and assigns their name and values into an array

current($array)
key($array)
next($array)
prev($array)
end($array)
reset($array)

All of these functions are specific to the internal pointer of an array, and in most cases are used in conjunction with one another. They are all included here at once to give clarity to how they work together.
current() – Returns the current entry's value; does not change the pointer
key() – Returns the current entry's key; does not change the pointer

15 The *prefix* is always appended by an underscore (_)

next() – Advances the pointer forward one, then returns the entry's value[16]
prev() – Rewinds the pointer backward one, then returns the entry's value[16]
end() – Advances the pointer to the end of the array, then returns the value
reset() – Rewinds the pointer to the beginning, then returns the entry's value

Examples:

```
$array = array( 'zero', 'one', 'two', 'three', 'four' );
echo current($array), ', ';   // returns: zero
echo key($array),     ', ';   // returns: 0
echo next($array),    ', ';   // returns: one
echo current($array), ', ';   // returns: one
echo end($array),     ', ';   // returns: four
echo prev($array),    ', ';   // returns: three
echo current($array), ', ';   // returns: three
echo reset($array);           // returns: zero
```

```
zero, 0, one, one, four, three, three, zero
```

See Also:

each() – Returns an array with the current key and value, and advances the pointer

each($array)

Returns an array containing the key and value of the current entry according to the internal pointer of **$array**. Returns FALSE if the current position of the internal pointer when **each()** is called is past the end of the array.
Note: *The returned array contains four entries, see below for the example.*

Examples:

```
$array = array( 'key' => 'value' );
$entry = each($array);
print_r($entry);
```

```
Array
(
    [1] => value
    [value] => value
    [0] => key
    [key] => key
)
```

```
$array = array( 'name' => 'Victor' );
$entry = each($array);
print_r($entry);
```

```
Array
(
 [1] => Victor
 [value] => Victor
 [0] => name
 [key] => name
)
```

16 If there are no more elements, function returns FALSE

list(*variable_name* [, ...*variable_name*...])

Accepts multiple variable_names

Assigns a list of variables with *variable_name* as the variable itself. Written in much the same way as assigning a value to a single variable, however the assigned value must be an array as the source, strings are not accepted.

Examples:

```
list($name) = 'Bob'; // Not an acceptable value, a string
var_dump($name);
```

```
NULL
```

```
$array = array('Bob');
list($name) = $array;
var_dump($name);
```

```
string(3) "Bob"
```

```
$array = array('Bob', 65, 'CEO');
list($name, $age, $title) = $array;
echo "$name ($title) - $age";
```

```
Bob (CEO) - 65
```

```
$array = array('Bob', 65, 'CEO');
list($name[], $name[], $name[]) = $array; // Assigned in reverse order
print_r($name);
```

```
Array ( [0] => CEO [1] => 65 [2] => Bob )
```

See Also:

array_values() – Returns all the values in an array

range(*start, end* [, *increment*])

start – **$integer**, **$float** or **$string** (single character)
end – **$integer**, **$float** or **$string** (single character)
increment – [optional] **$integer** or **$float**[17] *default:* 1

Returns an indexed array containing all the values between *start* and *end*, optionally incremented by *increment*. Incrementation of characters is based on their ASCII value code.
Note: *Start and end must be of the same variable type.*

Examples:

```
print_r( range(0, 3) );
```

```
Array ( [0] => 0 [1] => 1 [2] => 2 [3] => 3 )
```

```
print_r( range(2, 8, 2) );
```

```
Array ( [0] => 2 [1] => 4 [2] => 6 [3] => 8 )
```

17 Only available when *start* and *end* are integers or floats

```
print_r( range('m', 'o') );
```

```
Array ( [0] => m [1] => n [2] => o )
```

```
print_r( range('X', 'b') );
```

```
Array ( [0] => X [1] => Y [2] => Z [3] => [ [4] => \ [5] => ] [6] => ^
[7] => _ [8] => ` [9] => a [10] => b )
```

See Also:

array_fill() – Fills an array with a single value specified with a range of keys

http_build_query($array [, *prefix*] [, *separator*])

prefix – [optional] **$string**, should be included if **$array** is indexed, not associative
separator – [optional] *default:* ampersand (&)

Returns a query string from **$array** with key => value equivalent to key=value in the query string. If the array is indexed and not associative, this may cause problems for PHP since the key cannot be the name of a variable because it does not start with a letter or underscore, thus *prefix* should be included.

Examples:

```
$array = array( 'name' => 'Bob', 'title' => 'CEO', 'age' => '30' );
echo http_build_query($array);
```

```
name=Bob&title=CEO&age=30
```

```
$array = array( 'Bob', 'Jack', 'Tom' );
echo http_build_query($array, '_'); // prefix is an underscore ( _ )
```

```
_0=Bob&_1=Jack&_2=Tom
```

array_fill(*start, total, value*)

start – **$integer**
total – **$integer**
value – **$variable**

Returns an indexed array where the first key used is *start*, and *total* number of keys are created in order, all filled with *value*.

Example:

```
print_r( array_fill(0, 3, 'value') );
```

```
Array
(
    [0] => value
    [1] => value
    [2] => value
)
```

See Also:

range() – Fills an indexed array with a range of characters or numbers
array_fill_keys() – Fills an associative array with a specific value

array_fill_keys($array, *value*)

value – **$variable**

Returns an associative array where the keys of the new array are the values of **$array**, with the new array's vales set with *value*.

Example:

```
$array = array( 'key', 'name' );
print_r( array_fill_keys($array, 'value') );
```

```
Array
(
    [key] => value
    [name] => value
)
```

See Also:

array_fill() – Fills an array with a single value specified with a range of keys

array_pad($array, *size, value*)

size – **$integer**
value – **$variable**

Returns an array that has at least *size* entries, using the entries of **$array.** If *size* is not yet met, *value* is added as the value of indexed entries. If *size* is positive, entries are added at the end of the array. If *size* is negative, entries are added at the beginning of the array and the array is reindexed.

Example:

```
$array = array( 'zero', 'one' );
$padded_array = array_pad($array, 3, 'value');
print_r($padded_array);
```

```
Array
(
    [0] => zero
    [1] => one
    [2] => value
)
```

```
$array = array( 'zero', 'one' );
$padded_array = array_pad($array, -3, 'value');
print_r($padded_array);
```

```
Array
(
    [0] => value
    [1] => zero
    [2] => one
)
```

natsort($array)

Sorts the values of **$array** using more natural/human sorting.

Example:

```
$array = array('img4.jpg', 'img41.jpg', 'img3.jpg', 'img11.jpg');
echo 'Standard sort:<br />';
sort($array);
print_r($array);
echo 'Natural sort:<br />';
natsort($array);
print_r($array);
```

```
Standard sort:
Array
(
    [0] => img11.jpg
    [1] => img3.jpg
    [2] => img4.jpg
    [3] => img41.jpg
)
Natural sort:
Array
(
    [1] => img3.jpg
    [2] => img4.jpg
    [0] => img11.jpg
    [3] => img41.jpg
)
```

See Also:

natcasesort() – Case-insensitive version of **natsort()**
sort() – Sort the values of an array

natcasesort($array)

Sorts the values of **$array** using more natural/human sorting, case-insensitive.

Example:

```
$array = array('img4.jpg', 'IMG41.jpg', 'img11.jpg');
echo 'Standard sort:<br />';
sort($array);
print_r($array);
echo 'Natural sort:<br />';
natsort($array);
print_r($array);
echo 'Natural case-insensitive sort:<br />';
```

```
natcasesort($array);
print_r($array);
```

```
Standard sort:
Array
(
    [0] => IMG41.jpg
    [1] => img11.jpg
    [2] => img4.jpg
)
Natural sort:
Array
(
    [0] => IMG41.jpg
    [2] => img4.jpg
    [1] => img11.jpg
)
Natural case-insensitive sort:
Array
(
    [2] => img4.jpg
    [1] => img11.jpg
    [0] => IMG41.jpg
)
```

See Also:

natsort() – Case-sensitive version of **natcasesort()**
sort() – Sort the values of an array

Date/Time Functions

checkdate(*month, day, year*)

month – **$integer** (1-12)
day – **$integer** (1-31, varies)
year – **$integer** (1-32767)

Checks the validity of the given date, returning TRUE if it is valid.

Example:

```
var_dump( checkdate(2, 29, 2006) );
```

```
bool(false)
```

```
var_dump( checkdate(2, 29, 2008) );
```

```
bool(true)
```

date(*format* [, *timestamp*])

format – **$string**
timestamp – [optional] **$integer** *default:* **time()**, current Unix timestamp

Returns the current date and/or time based on formatting specified in *format*. If *timestamp* is not included, the current time is used, supplied by the **time()** function. Otherwise, the supplied *timestamp* is evaluated instead.
The following options are available for *format*:

- Day

  d – *(01 – 31)* Day of the month with leading zeros
  j – *(1 – 31)* Day of the month without leading zeros
  D – *(Mon – Sun)* Three letter version of the day of the week
  l (lowercase 'L') – (*Sunday – Saturday)* Day of the week, full word
  N – (1 – 7) Day of the week ISO-8601, numerical Monday(1) – Sunday(7)
  w – (0 – 6) Day of the week, numerical Sunday (0) – Saturday (6)
  S – (st,nd,rd,th) Suffix for day of the month, used with *j*
  z – (0 – 365) Day of the year

- Week

  W – (01 – 52) Week of the year

- Month

  F – (January – December) Month, full word
  M – (Jan – Dec) Three letter version of the month
  m – (01 – 12) Month, numerical with leading zeros
  n – (1 – 12) Month, numerical without leading zeros
  t – (28 – 31) Number of days in the month

- Year

  L – (1 or 0) Whether it is (1) or is not (0) leap year
  Y – (2008) Four digit representation of the year
  y – (08) Two digit representation of the year
  o – (2008) ISO-8601 version of 'Y', affected by the week ('W')

- Time

  a – (am or pm) Lowercase ante meridiem or post meridiem
  A – (AM or PM) Uppercase ante meridiem or post meridiem
  B – (000 – 999) Swatch internet time
  g – (1 – 12) 12-hour format of the hour, without leading zeros
  h – (01 – 12) 12-hour format of the hour, with leading zeros
  G – (0 – 23) 24-hour format of the hour, without leading zeros
  H – (00 – 23) 24-hour format of the hour, with leading zeros
  i – (00 – 59) Minutes with leading zeros
  s – (00 – 59) Seconds with leading zeros
  u – (*e.g.* 54321) Milliseconds

- Timezone

  e – (*e.g.* GMT, America/Denver) Full timezone identifier
  T - (*e.g.* GMT, EST, PST) Timezone abbreviation
  I – (1 or 0) Whether it is (1) daylight saving time or not (0)
  O - (*e.g.* -0700) Difference to GMT in hours
  P - (*e.g.* -07:00) Difference to GMT in hours with the added colon
  Z - (-43200 – 50400) Timezone offset in seconds, negative for west of UTC

- Full Date/Time

  c – (*e.g.* 2008-03-17T12:27:40-06:00) ISO-8601 formatted date
  r – (*e.g.* Mon, 17 Mar 2008 12:27:40 -0600) RFC 2822 date
  U – (*e.g.* 1205778601) Time since Unix Epoch, same as **time()**

Examples:

```
echo date('m-d-y');
```

```
03-17-08
```

```
echo date('M jS, Y');
```

```
Mar 17th, 2008
```

```
echo date('g:i:sA');
```

```
12:27:40PM
```

See Also:

time() – Get the current Unix timestamp, time since Unix Epoch
strtotime() - Convert a common language string to a Unix timestamp

When using **date()**, be careful about including extraneous characters. Any character that is listed previously as a formatting character but should be output literally needs to be escaped with a backslash (\ ).

```
// Unexpected results
echo date('m-d-Y, WS week');
```

```
03-17-2008, 12th 1America/DenverAmerica/Denverk
```

```
// Same thing, with escaped characters
echo date('m-d-Y, WS \w\e\ek');
```

```
03-17-2008, 12th week
```

```
// Better way with concatenation
echo date('m-d-Y, WS') . ' week';
```

```
03-17-2008, 12th week
```

gmdate(*format* [, *timestamp*])

format – **$string**
timestamp – [optional] **$integer** *default:* **time()**, current Unix timestamp

Returns the current date and/or time based on formatting specified in *format* returned in GMT/UTC. If *timestamp* is not included, the current time is used, supplied by the **time()** function. Otherwise, the supplied *timestamp* is evaluated instead. See **date()** for formatting.
Note: *Formatting character 'Z' will always return 0 when used with* ***gmdate()****.*

Example:

```
echo gmdate('M jS, Y e');
```

```
Mar 17th, 2008 UTC
```

See Also:

date() – Performs the same function without the GMT/UTC restriction

getdate([*timestamp*])

timestamp – [optional] **$integer** *default:* **time()**, current Unix timestamp

Returns an associative array containing all of the information about the current date/time or instead the *timestamp* if it is supplied.

Example:

```
print_r( getdate() );
```

```
Array
(
    [seconds] => 39
    [minutes] => 3
    [hours] => 13
    [mday] => 17
    [wday] => 1
    [mon] => 3
    [year] => 2008
    [yday] => 76
    [weekday] => Monday
    [month] => March
    [0] => 1205780619
)
```

time()

Returns the current Unix timestamp in seconds since the Unix Epoch (January 1st, 1970, 00:00:00 GMT) as an integer.

Example:

```
var_dump( time() );
```

```
int(1205780960)
```

See Also:

mktime() – Similar function, but accepts specific date/time arguments
date() – Formats the Unix timestamp to a human readable format

mktime([, *hour*] [, *minute*] [, *second*] [, *month*] [, *day*] [, *year*] [, *dst_flag*])

hour – [optional] **$integer**
minute – [optional] **$integer**
second – [optional] **$integer**
month – [optional] **$integer**
day – [optional] **$integer**
year – [optional] **$integer**
dst_flag – [optional] **$integer** *default:* -1, daylight saving time status unknown
Other values: 0, not in daylight saving time
1, in daylight saving time

Returns the current Unix timestamp in seconds since the Unix Epoch (January 1st, 1970, 00:00:00 GMT) as an integer. However, it takes optional arguments for a specific date/time. Optional arguments can be left off from right to left, anything not included will default to the current date/time. **Note:** *The dst_flag is not the best way of handing daylight saving time; timezone specific functions are recommended instead in PHP5. It is left here as reference, since the extended timezone specific functions are outside of the scope of this book.*

Example:

```
var_dump( mktime(1,23,40,3,17,2008) );
```

```
int(1205738620)
```

See Also:

time() – Generates the Unix timestamp for the current time only

gmmktime([, *hour*] [, *minute*] [, *second*] [, *month*] [, *day*] [, *year*] [, *dst_flag*])

hour, minute, second, month, day, and *year* – [optional] **$integer**
dst_flag – [optional] **$integer** *default:* -1, daylight saving time status unknown
Other values: 0, not in daylight saving time
1, in daylight saving time

Returns the current GMT Unix timestamp in seconds since the Unix Epoch (January 1st, 1970, 00:00:00 GMT) as an integer. However, it takes optional arguments for a specific date/time. Optional arguments can be left off from right to left, anything not included will default to the current date/time. **Note:** *The dst_flag is not the best way of handing daylight saving time; timezone specific functions are recommended instead in PHP5. It is left here as reference, since the extended timezone specific functions are outside of the scope of this book.*

Example:

```
var_dump( gmmktime(1,23,40,3,17,2008) );
```

```
int(1205717020)
```

See Also:

mktime() – Performs the same function, but without the GMT restriction

microtime([*float_flag*])

float_flag – [optional] **$boolean** *default:* FALSE, returns a string

Returns the current Unix timestamp with microseconds. By default, it returns a string in the format: '*microseconds seconds*'. If *float_flag* is set to TRUE, it returns the value as a float.

Examples:

```
var_dump( microtime() );
```

```
string(21) "0.33776600 1205782759"
```

```
var_dump( microtime(TRUE) ); // Can also be written as microtime(1)
```

```
float(1205782778.02)
```

See Also:

time() – Returns the current Unix timestamp in seconds

If you want to know how long it took to complete a script, for instance when comparing two different functions to see which is faster, you can use **microtime()** to track the efficiency.

```
$start = microtime(1);
// Do something here
$end = microtime(1);
$lengthoftime = number_format($end - $start, 6);
echo "It took $lengthoftime seconds to run this script.";
```

```
It took 0.000005 seconds to run this script.
```

strtotime($string [, *timestamp*])

timestamp – [optional]**$integer** *default:* **time()**

Returns the Unix timestamp based on the interpretation of the date/time in **$string**, which is a common language format of the date/time. If **$string** is a relative input format that refers to a date (*e.g.* 'last month'), the current date/time is used unless the optional *timestamp* is supplied. Returns FALSE if **$string** is not valid and the function fails.

Examples:

```
$result = strtotime('December 8th, 1941');
echo $result;
echo '<br />'; // XHTML line break
echo date('r', $result);
```

```
-885661200
Mon, 08 Dec 1941 00:00:00 -0700
```

```
$result = strtotime('26apr86');
echo date('r', $result);
```

```
Sat, 26 Apr 1986 00:00:00 -0700
```

```
$result = strtotime('20010911 08:45:00');
echo date('r', $result);
```

```
Tue, 11 Sep 2001 08:45:00 -0600
```

Relative $string examples:

```
$result = strtotime('last week'); // This time, last week
echo date('r', $result);
```

```
Mon, 10 Mar 2008 14:31:54 -0600
```

```
$date = mktime(8,45,00,9,11,2001); // Sept. 11, 2001 8:45am
$result = strtotime('next week', $date);
echo date('r', $result);
```

```
Tue, 18 Sep 2001 08:45:00 -0600
```

```
$date = mktime(8,45,00,9,11,2001); // Sept. 11, 2001 8:45am
$result = strtotime('+2 friday', $date);
echo date('r', $result);
```

```
Fri, 21 Sep 2001 00:00:00 -0600
```

```
$result = strtotime('1 hour ago');
echo date('r', $result);
```

```
Mon, 17 Mar 2008 13:36:54 -0600
```

```
$result = strtotime('yesterday 3am');
echo date('r', $result);
```

```
Sun, 16 Mar 2008 03:00:00 -0600
```

```
$result = strtotime('7am 4 days ago');
echo date('r', $result);
```

```
Thu, 13 Mar 2008 07:00:00 -0600
```

There are many more examples. Please see the following websites:
http://www.gnu.org/software/tar/manual/html_node/tar_113.html
http://www.phpdig.net/ref/rn13re206.html

See Also:

date() – Convert the Unix timestamp to a more human readable format

The power of this function is not only to convert common language into something usable without an endless string of regular expressions, but also when working with relative dates and times. If pulling data from a database using MySQL queries to generate a report of all calls in the previous week (Monday through Friday), you would have to go through a lot of calculations to figure out what day it is today, then based on that figure out what the date was on Monday, then submit the proper query. With this function, you can quickly find the two dates without the extra math, it's done for you!

Mathematical Functions

Sometimes you need more advanced mathematics.

abs(*number*)

number – **$integer** or **$float**

Returns the absolute value of *number* as the same variable type.

Example:

```
var_dump( abs(-21) );
```

```
int(21)
```

dechex($integer)

Returns the hexadecimal value of **$integer**. Maximum number: 4294967295.

Example:

```
var_dump( dechex(4294967295) );
```

```
string(8) "ffffffff"
```

max($array)
max($variable, $variable [, ...$variable...])

Depending on the arguments supplied, there are two different formats

If supplied a single argument, **$array**, it returns the highest value in the array.
If supplied two or more **$variable**, it returns the highest value argument.[18]
Note: *Non-numeric strings are evaluated as zero (0) for comparison purposes.*

Examples:

```
$array = array(4, 7, 2);
var_dump( max($array) );
```

```
int(7)
```

18 If comparing two arrays, they are evaluated value vs value, left to right

```
var_dump( max(2, 5, 'string', '8') );
```

```
string(1) "8"
```

See Also:

min() – Finds the lowest value

min($array)
min($variable, $variable [, ...$variable...])

Depending on the arguments supplied, there are two different formats

If supplied a single argument, **$array**, it returns the highest value in the array.
If supplied two or more **$variable**, it returns the lowest value argument.[19]
Note: *Non-numeric strings are evaluated as zero (0) for comparison purposes.*

Examples:

```
$array = array(-3, 7, 2);
var_dump( min($array) );
```

```
int(-3)
```

```
var_dump( min( array(1,2,3), array(1,2,4) ) ); // 1==1, 2==2, 3<4
```

```
array(3) { [0]=> int(1) [1]=> int(2) [2]=> int(3) }
```

See Also:

max() – Finds the highest value

pi()

Returns an approximation of pi as a float.

Example:

```
var_dump( pi() );
```

```
float(3.14159265359)
```

pow(*base, exponent*)

base – **$integer** or **$float**
exponent – **$integer** or **$float**

Returns the value of *base* raised to the power of *exponent*.

Example:

```
var_dump( pow(2, 4) );
```

```
int(16)
```

19 If comparing two arrays, they are evaluated value vs value, left to right

sqrt($float)

Returns the square root of **$float**.

Example:

```
var_dump( sqrt(16) );
```

```
float(4)
```

log($float [, *base*])

base – [optional] **$float**

Returns the natural logarithm of **$float**. The optional *base* is presented as follows:
$\log_{base}$ **$float**

Example:

```
var_dump( log(10) );
```

```
float(2.30258509299)
```

round($float [, *decimals*])

decimals – [optional] **$integer** *default:* 0 decimal places

Rounds up the **$float** to the nearest integer. If *decimals* is specified, it is rounded to *decimals* number of decimal places[20].

Examples:

```
var_dump( round(3.14) );
```

```
float(3)
```

```
var_dump( round(pi(), 2) );
```

```
float(3.14)
```

```
var_dump( round(143257.432, -2) );
```

```
float(143300)
```

See Also:

floor() – Rounds down to the nearest integer instead of rounding up

20 If *decimals* is negative, it will round that many places to the left of the decimal place

floor($float)

Rounds down **$float** to the nearest integer.

Example:

```
var_dump( floor(3.99) );
```

```
float(3)
```

See Also:

round() – Rounds up to the nearest integer or decimal place

rand([*min, max*])

min, max – [optional] **$integers**

Generates a random integer. For better randomization, use **mt_rand()** instead.

Example:

```
var_dump( rand(), rand(1,100) ); // Results vary
```

```
int(1620708157) int(63)
```

See Also:

mt_rand() – A better and faster random number generator

mt_rand([*min, max*])

min, max – [optional] **$integers**

Generates a random integer, better than **rand()**. If supplied, it will generate a random integer between *min* and *max*.

Example:

```
var_dump( mt_rand(), mt_rand(1,100) ); // Results vary
```

```
int(931438462) int(25)
```

MySQL Functions

Ah databases. In one form or another, if you want to store data and retrieve it in an efficient manner, you probably will use a database. The popular MySQL database is part of the LAMP stack (Linux-Apache-MySQL-PHP) and deserves a little attention and explanation. Be aware, with the exception of a few examples, this section explains PHP functions, not how to build MySQL queries.

Note: *MySQL* ***5*** *is assumed. Some queries listed here will not work in MySQL 4.*

MySQL data types

type – max value (signed/unsigned)
TINYINT – 127 / 255
SMALLINT – 32,767 / 65,535
MEDIUMINT – 8,388,607 / 16,777,215
INT – 2,147,483,647 / 4,294,967,295
BIGINT – 9,223,372,036,854,775,807 / 18,446,744,073,709,551,615

date/time formats
DATE format: YYYY-MM-DD
TIME format: HH:MM:SS
DATETIME format: YYYY-MM-DD HH:MM:SS
TIMESTAMP format: YYYY-MM-DD HH:MM:SS and auto-updates now()
Alternate forms for datetime/timestamp: YYYYMMDDHHMMSS

type – max length
CHAR() – 255, fixed
VARCHAR() – 255, variable
TINYTEXT – 255
TEXT / BLOB – 65,535
MEDIUMTEXT / MEDIUMBLOB – 16,777,215
LONGTEXT / LONGBLOB – 4,294,967,295

MySQL Query Basics

The following table will be used to demonstrate these queries:

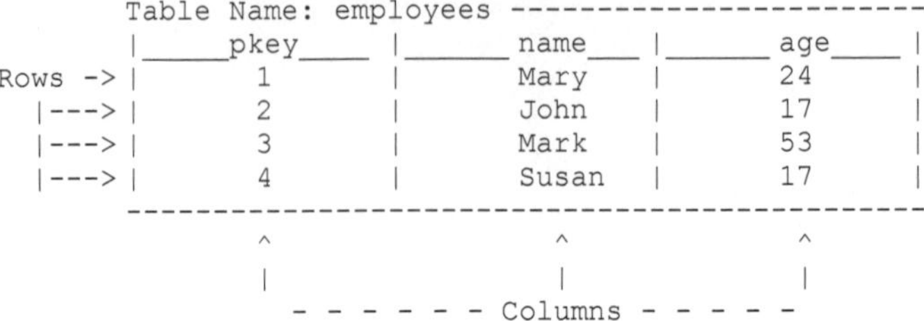
```
          Table Name: employees -----------------------
          |_____pkey____ |______ name___ |______ age____ |
Rows -> |       1        |       Mary    |       24      |
   |---> |       2        |       John    |       17      |
   |---> |       3        |       Mark    |       53      |
   |---> |       4        |       Susan   |       17      |
          ---------------------------------------------
                  ^                ^                ^
                  |                |                |
              - - - - - - Columns - - - - -
```

Examples:

```
SELECT * FROM employees
// Everything is returned
SELECT pkey,name,age FROM employees
// Everything is returned
SELECT employees.pkey,employees.name,employees.age FROM table
// Everything is returned
SELECT name FROM employees
// Everything in name column: Mary, John, Mark, Susan
SELECT name,age FROM employees
// Name and age columns: Mary,24 - John,17 - Mark,53 - Susan,17
SELECT * FROM employees WHERE age = 17
// Returns two rows: 2,John,17 - 4,Susan,17
SELECT name FROM employees WHERE name LIKE 'm%'
// Returns two names: Mary and Mark
SELECT name FROM employees WHERE name LIKE BINARY 'm%'
// Returns an empty result because it is a case-sensitive search
SELECT name FROM employees WHERE name LIKE '%a%'
// Returns three names: Mary, Mark, and Susan
SELECT name FROM employees WHERE name LIKE '_____' // 5 underscores
// Returns one name: Susan
SELECT COUNT(*) FROM employees
/ Returns the number of rows: 4
SELECT COUNT(*) FROM employees WHERE age = 17
// Returns: 2
SELECT age,COUNT(age) FROM employees GROUP BY age
// Returns three rows (age,count(age)): 17,2 - 24,1 - 53,1
SELECT SUM(age) FROM employees
// Returns sum of values in age: 111
```

```
SELECT MAX(age) FROM employees
```

```
// Returns: 53
```

```
SELECT DISTINCT age FROM employees
```

```
// Returns all unique values in age: 24, 17, 53
```

```
SELECT * FROM employees LIMIT 1,2
```

```
// Returns results starting with 1 (rows start with 0), for 2 length
// Returns 2 rows: 2,John,17 and 3,Mark,53
```

```
SELECT name FROM employees ORDER BY name
```

```
// Returns name column sorted ascending by name: John,Mark,Mary,Susan
```

```
SELECT name FROM employees ORDER BY name DESC
```

```
// Returns name column sorted descending by name: Susan,Mary,Mark,John
```

The following examples do not use the included table and are for reference only:

```
INSERT INTO table (column1,column2) VALUES ('value1','value2'),
('value1','value2'), ('value1','value2')
```

```
// Inserts the supplied values into the specific columns
```

```
UPDATE table SET column1='newvalue' WHERE column2='value'
```

```
// Updates all rows in table when WHERE condition is matched with the
// newvalue in column1 (column1 and column2 could be the same column)
```

```
DELETE FROM table WHERE column='value'
```

```
// Delete any rows in table where the condition is met
```

```
SELECT * FROM table1 INNER JOIN table2 on table1.id = table2.id
```

```
// Returns all columns in table1 and table2 where the id matches
// on both tables (any rows in table1 without an id that matches
// is excluded from the resulting combined results)
```

```
SELECT table1.* FROM table1 INNER JOIN table2 on table1.id = table2.id
```

```
// Same as above, except only columns from table1 are included
```

```
SELECT table1.id FROM table1 INNER JOIN table2 on table1.id = table2.id
```

```
// Same as above, except only the id column from table1 is included
```

```
SELECT table.id AS tableid FROM table
```

```
// Give an alias to the column using AS (so id will result as tableid)
```

mysql_connect([, *server*] [, *username*] [, *password*] [, *new_link*] [, *client_flag*])

server – [optional] **$string** *default:* 'localhost:3306' or *mysql.default_host*
username – [optional] **$string** *default:* defined by *mysql.default_user*
password – [optional] **$string** *default:* defined by *mysql.default_password*
new_link – [optional] **$boolean** *default:* FALSE, no new link on second call
client_flag – [optional] **$integer**

Establishes the initial connection/link to the MySQL server located at *server* and using the permissions provided by the *username* and *password*. Returns

FALSE on failure and should be combined with **die()** for security purposes. In most cases, you will use: **mysql_connect(***server, username, password***)**.

Example:

```
mysql_connect('localhost', 'user', 'password') or die('Could not
connect to the database');
```

See Also:

die() – Halts the script when the function fails
mysql_close() – Closes the connection to the database

mysql_close([*link_identifier*])

link_identifier – [optional] *default:* last link opened

Closes the connection to the MySQL server, by default, of the last connection by **mysql_connect()**. If *link_identifier* is specified, that link is closed instead.

Example:

```
$link = mysql_connect('localhost', 'username', 'password') or die();
$link2 = mysql_connect('/path/to', 'username', 'password') or die();
mysql_close($link); // Closes first link
mysql_close(); // Closes the last link created, $link2 in this case
```

See Also:

mysql_connect() – Establish a connection to the MySQL server

mysql_select_db(*database* [, *link_identifier*])

database – **$string**
link_identifier – [optional] *default:* last link opened

Selects the database to use specified by the name *database*. By default, it uses the most recent MySQL server connection by **mysql_connect()**, unless *link_identifier* is specified, then that link is used instead.

Example:

```
$link = mysql_connect('localhost', 'username', 'password') or die();
mysql_select_db('database'); // or mysql_select_db('database',$link);
```

See Also:

mysql_connect() – Establish a connection to the MySQL server

mysql_query(*query* [, *link_identifier*])

query – **$string**
link_identifier – [optional] *default:* last link opened

Submits *query* to the server, using the most recent **mysql_connect()** link unless the optional *link_identifier* is specified. Returns FALSE on any errors in the query. SELECT, SHOW, DESCRIBE, and EXPLAIN queries will return a resource that will need to be parsed by one of the **mysql_result()** or **mysql_fetch_*()** functions, all other queries will return TRUE upon success.

Example:

```
mysql_connect('localhost', 'username', 'password') or die();
mysql_select_db('database');
$result = mysql_query("SELECT * FROM 'table'");
```

See Also:

mysql_fetch_array() – Get a row as an array from the resource created
mysql_fetch_assoc() – Returns an associative array: column=>value
mysql_fetch_row() – Returns an indexed array of the row
mysql_result() - Get a single result from the resource created

mysql_db_query(*database*, *query* [, *link_identifier*])

database – **$string**
query – **$string**
link_identifier – [optional] *default:* last link opened

Sends *query* to the MySQL server and *database*.
Listed for reference, use **mysql_select_db()** and **mysql_query()** instead.

Example:

```
$result = mysql_db_query('database', "SELECT * FROM 'table'");
```

See Also:

mysql_select_db() – Select the database to connect to
mysql_query() - Send a query to the server

mysql_error([*link_identifier*])

link_identifier – [optional] *default:* last link opened

Returns the MySQL error of the last MySQL operation by default, or if specified, the *link_identifier*.

Example:

```
$link = mysql_connect('localhost', 'user', 'password'); // Valid
mysql_select_db('NoPermission');
echo mysql_error();
```

```
Access denied for user 'user'@'localhost' to database 'NoPermission'
```

mysql_fetch_array(*resource* [, *result_type*])

resource – Variable name containing the output of **mysql_query()**
result_type – [optional] **$string** *default:* MYSQL_BOTH
Values: MYSQL_BOTH (array with both associative and numeric)
MYSQL_ASSOC (array with associative indices)
MYSQL_NUM (array with numeric indices)

Returns an array with a single row of the *resource* generated from **mysql_query()** and advances the resource's internal pointer to the next row. This is typically used in a loop to extract all rows of the resource and get the entire output of the query. By default, it provides both the associative and numeric indices, but this can be altered by *result_type*.

Example:

```
//nametable:    |pkey| name |
//              |----|------|
// Row 0:       | 3  | Mark |
// Row 1:       | 2  | John |
$result = mysql_query("SELECT * FROM nametable");
$array = mysql_fetch_array($result);
print_r($array);
$array = mysql_fetch_array($result,MYSQL_ASSOC);
print_r($array);
```

```
Array
(
    [0] => 3
    [pkey] => 3
    [1] => Mark
    [name] => Mark
)
Array
(
    [pkey] => 2
    [name] => John
)
```

Example using a loop and MYSQL_NUM option:

```
$result = mysql_query("SELECT * FROM nametable");
while ($row = mysql_fetch_array($result, MYSQL_NUM) ){
    print_r($row);
}
```

```
Array
(
    [0] => 3
    [1] => Mark
```

```
)

Array
(
    [0] => 2
    [1] => John
)
```

See Also:

mysql_fetch_assoc() – Equivalent to mysql_fetch_array(*result*, MYSQL_ASSOC)
mysql_fetch_row() – Equivalent to mysql_fetch_array(*result*, MYSQL_NUM)

mysql_fetch_assoc(*resource*)

resource – Variable name containing the output of **mysql_query()**

Returns an array with a single row of the *resource* generated from **mysql_query()** and advances the resource's internal pointer to the next row, returning an associative array with column => value association.

Example:

```
//nametable:    |pkey| name |
//              |----|------|
// Row 0:       | 3  | Mark |
// Row 1:       | 2  | John |
$result = mysql_query("SELECT * FROM nametable");
$array = mysql_fetch_assoc($result);
print_r($array);
// If you were to repeat the last 2 lines, you would get row 1 instead
```

```
Array
(
    [pkey] => 3
    [name] => Mark
)
```

Example using a while loop:

```
$result = mysql_query("SELECT * FROM nametable");
while ($row = mysql_fetch_assoc($result) ){
    print_r($row);
}
```

```
Array
(
    [pkey] => 3
    [name] => Mark
)
Array
(
    [pkey] => 2
    [name] => John
)
```

See Also:

mysql_fetch_array() – Similar, but can return both associative and indexed
mysql_fetch_row() – Similar, but returns an indexed array

mysql_fetch_row(*resource*)

resource – Variable name containing the output of **mysql_query()**

Returns an array with a single row of the *resource* generated from **mysql_query()** and advances the resource's internal pointer to the next row, returning an indexed array with only the values (no column names).

Example:

```
//nametable:    |pkey| name |
//              |----|------|
// Row 0:       | 3  | Mark |
// Row 1:       | 2  | John |
$result = mysql_query("SELECT * FROM nametable");
$array = mysql_fetch_row($result);
print_r($array);
// If you were to repeat the last 2 lines, you would get row 1 instead
```

```
Array
(
    [0] => 3
    [1] => Mark
)
```

Example using a while loop:

```
$result = mysql_query("SELECT * FROM nametable");
while ($row = mysql_fetch_row($result) ){
    print_r($row);
}
```

```
Array
(
    [0] => 3
    [1] => Mark
)
Array
(
    [0] => 2
    [1] => John
)
```

See Also:

mysql_fetch_array() – Similar, but can return both associative and indexed
mysql_fetch_assoc() – Similar, but returns an associative array: column=>value

mysql_result(*resource, row* [, *column*])

resource – Variable name containing the output of **mysql_query()**
row – **$integer**
column – [optional] **$string or $integer** *default:* 0, first column is retrieved

Returns a string containing a single cell from a specific *row* of the *resource* generated from **mysql_query()**. If *field* is specified, instead of the value of the first column, the specified *field* is retrieved (can be referenced by number starting with 0 or by name/alias).
Note: *If you need more than a single result, you should use a mysql_fetch_*()*

Examples:

```
//nametable:    |pkey| name |
//              |----|------|
// Row 0:       | 3  | Mark |
// Row 1:       | 2  | John |
$result = mysql_query("SELECT * FROM nametable");
var_dump( mysql_result($result, 0) );
var_dump( mysql_result($result, 1) );
```

```
string(1) "3"
string(1) "2"
```

```
var_dump( mysql_result($result, 0, 1) );
var_dump( mysql_result($result, 1, 'name') );
```

```
string(4) "Mark"
string(4) "John"
```

See Also:

mysql_fetch_array() – Returns both associative and indexed array of the row
mysql_fetch_assoc() – Returns an associative array: column=>value
mysql_fetch_row() – Returns an indexed array of the row

mysql_num_rows(*resource*)

resource – Variable name containing the output of **mysql_query()**

Returns the total number of rows in the *resource* generated by **mysql_query()** as an integer.

Example:

```
//nametable:    |pkey| name |
//              |----|------|
// Row 0:       | 3  | Mark |
// Row 1:       | 2  | John |
$result = mysql_query("SELECT * FROM nametable");
$row_total = mysql_num_rows($result);
var_dump($row_total);
```

```
int(2)
```

mysql_free_result(*resource*)

resource – Variable name containing the output of **mysql_query()**

Clears the system memory of all memory associated with *resource*. Only necessary if working with large data sets within a single script, memory is automatically cleared at the end of the script/page.

Example:

```
$result = mysql_query("SELECT * FROM nametable");
var_dump( mysql_free_result($result) );
```

```
bool(true)
```

mysql_get_server_info([*link_identifier*])

link_identifier – [optional] *default:* last link opened

Returns a string with the MySQL server version, by default, of the last connection by **mysql_connect()**. If *link_identifier* is specified, that link is used instead.

Example:

```
$link = mysql_connect('localhost', 'username', 'password') or die();
var_dump( mysql_get_server_info() ); // Results vary
```

```
string(7) "5.0.51a"
```

See Also:

mysql_connect() – Establish a connection to the MySQL server

mysql_real_escape_string($string [,*link_identifier*])

link_identifier – [optional] *default:* last link opened

Returns a string with the **$string** processed for any special characters, adding a backslash to escape the character and prevent SQL injection attacks. By default, the last connection by **mysql_connect()** is used. If *link_identifier* is specified, that link is used instead.
Effects the following characters: \x00, \n, \r, \, ', and ".
Note: *Performs the same functionality as* ***addslashes().***

Example:

```
$string = "SELECT * FROM 'table'";
mysql_connect('localhost', 'username', 'password') or die();
var_dump( mysql_real_escape_string($string) );
```

```
string(23) "SELECT * FROM \'table\'"
```

See Also:

addslashes() – Performs the same function, but without a database call
get_magic_quotes_gpc() – Checks for the PHP setting magic_quotes_gpc

mysql_data_seek(*resource, row*)

resource – Variable name containing the output of **mysql_query()**
row – **$integer**

Advances the internal pointer of *resource* generated by **mysql_query()** to row number *row* (starting with row 0). Thus, the next mysql_fetch_*() function request grabs the specified row number.

Example:

```
//nametable:    |pkey| name |
//              |----|------|
// Row 0:       | 3  | Mark |
// Row 1:       | 2  | John |
$result = mysql_query("SELECT * FROM nametable");
mysql_data_seek($result, 1); // Choose row 1
$array = mysql_fetch_array($result);
print_r($array);
```

```
Array
(
    [0] => 2
    [pkey] => 2
    [1] => John
    [name] => John
)
```

See Also:

mysql_fetch_array() – Returns both associative and indexed array of the row

mysql_affected_rows([*link_identifier*])

link_identifier – [optional] *default:* last link opened

Returns the number of rows affected by the last INSERT, UPDATE, DELETE, or REPLACE query. If *link_identifier* is specified, the last query associated with the specified **mysql_connect()** link is used.

Example:

```
//Table name:  |pkey| name |
// nametable   |----|------|
mysql_connect('localhost', 'username', 'password') or die();
mysql_select_db('database');
$result = mysql_query(" INSERT INTO nametable (pkey,name) VALUES
(NULL,'Joe') ");
var_dump( mysql_affected_rows() );
```

```
int(1)
```

mysql_create_db($string [, *link_identifier*])

link_identifier – [optional] *default:* last link opened

Creates a database with the name **$string** on the MySQL server last used with **mysql_connect()**, unless *link_identifier* is specified, then that one is used instead.
Note: *Reference only, use* ***mysql_query()*** *and "CREATE DATABASE"*

Example:

```
mysql_connect('localhost', 'username', 'password') or die();
mysql_create_db('database');
```

See Also:

mysql_query() – Send a query to the MySQL database

mysql_drop_db($string [, *link_identifier*])

link_identifier – [optional] *default:* last link opened

Destroys a database with the name **$string** on the MySQL server last used with **mysql_connect()**, unless *link_identifier* is specified, then that one is used instead.
Note: *Reference only, use* ***mysql_query()*** *and "DROP DATABASE"*

Example:

```
mysql_connect('localhost', 'username', 'password') or die();
mysql_drop_db('database');
```

See Also:

mysql_query() – Send a query to the MySQL database

Directory & File System Functions

getcwd()

Returns a string containing the current directory.

Example:

```
var_dump( getcwd() ); // Results will vary
```

```
string(17) "/opt/lampp/htdocs"
```

See Also:

chdir() – Changes the current directory

chdir($string)

Changes the current directory to **$string**, returning TRUE when successful. **Note:** *Directory change lasts only as long as the current script/page.*

Example:

```
var_dump( getcwd() ); // Get the current directory
chdir('images');
var_dump( getcwd() );
```

```
string(17) "/opt/lampp/htdocs/images"
```

See Also:

getcwd() – Get the current directory

scandir($string [, *sort_flag*])

sort_flag – [optional] $integer default: 0 (sort ascending)
Other value: 1 (sort descending)

Return an array containing all files and directories inside of the directory **$string**. If *sort_flag* is 0 or not specified, the array is sorted alphabetically in ascending order.

Example:

```
$array = scandir('directory'); // Results vary
print_r($array);
```

```
Array
(
    [0] => .
    [1] => ..
    [2] => anotherdirectory
    [3] => file.txt
    [4] => index.html
    [5] => test.php
)
```

copy(*source, destination*)

source – **$string**
destination – **$string**

Copies a file with name *source* to name *destination,* overwriting the *destination* file it if already exists. The original *source* file is unchanged.

Example:

```
copy('file.txt', 'file.txt.bak');
```

```
// Both file.txt and file.txt.bak now exist with the same contents
```

rename(*oldname, newname*)

oldname – **$string**
newname – **$string**

Rename the file or directory with the name *oldname* to the name *newname*.

Examples:

```
rename('file.txt', 'file.tmp');
```

```
// file.txt was renamed to file.tmp
```

```
rename('file.txt', 'tmp/file.tmp');
```

```
// file.txt was moved to the subdirectory 'tmp' and renamed to file.tmp
```

mkdir(*path* [*, nix_mode*] [*, recursive_flag*])

path – **$string**
nix_mode – [optional] **$integer** *default:* 0777 (octal), read/write for everyone[21]
recursive_flag – [optional] **$boolean** *default:* FALSE, one directory at a time

21 Does not effect Windows based servers, and if included, is ignored

Creates a directory at *path*. If on a Unix/Linux server, you can change the default *mode* from 0777 to other permissions in octal form (leading zero). Only one directory deep can be created at a time unless *recursive_flag* is set to TRUE.

Examples:

```
mkdir('tmp');
// Directory with the name 'tmp' is created
mkdir('tmp/tmp2/tmp3', 0775, TRUE);
// All three directories are created 'tmp', 'tmp/tmp2', 'tmp/tmp2/tmp3'
```

See Also:

chmod() – Change file mode (permissions)

rmdir($string)

Remove the directory with the path **$string**.

Example:

```
rmdir('/temp/tmp');
// Directory removed /temp/tmp
```

unlink($string)

Delete the file with the name/path **$string**.

Example:

```
unlink('file.txt');
// file.txt is deleted
```

fopen(*filename, mode* [, *use_include_path*])

filename – **$string**
mode – **$string**
use_include_path – [optional] **$boolean** *default:* FALSE

Opens a file with name *filename* using the following *mode*:

- 'r' (read only, file pointer at the beginning)
- 'r+' (read and write, file pointer at the beginning)
- 'w' (write only, file pointer at the beginning, zero length file, create it if it does not exist)

- 'w+' (read and write, file pointer at the beginning, zero length file, create it if it does not exist)
- 'a' (write only, file pointer at the end, zero length file)
- 'a+' (read and write, file pointer at the end, zero length file)
- 'x' (write only, file pointer at the beginning, if exists, return FALSE)
- 'x+' (read and write, file pointer at the beginning, if exists, return FALSE)

If *use_include_path* is set to TRUE, the system will check in the PHP defined include_path for the file as well. Returns a resource for the usage of other functions.

Example:

```
$file = fopen('file.txt', 'r');
```

```
// Resource is now stored as $file, and file.txt is open for read only
```

See Also:

fclose() – Closes the file and resource opened by **fopen()**

fclose(*resource*)

resource –Variable name containing the file pointer created by **fopen()**

Closes a file opened with **fopen()**.

Example:

```
$file = fopen('file.txt', 'r');
fclose($file);
```

See Also:

fopen() – Opens a file for reading, writing, or both

fread(*resource, length*)

resource –Variable name containing the file pointer created by **fopen()**
length – **$integer**

Returns a string containing the contents of *resource* created by **fopen()** for the byte length *length*.

Example:

```
// file.txt contains the sentence: Hello World!
$file = fopen('file.txt', 'r');
var_dump( fread($file, 8) );
```

```
string(8) "Hello Wo"
```

See Also:

fwrite() – Writes to the opened file
fopen() – Opens a file for reading, writing, or both

To read the entire file into a string, use the function **filesize()**.

```
// file.txt contains the sentence: Hello World!
$filename = 'file.txt';
$file = fopen($filename, 'r');
$string = fread( $file, filesize($filename) );
var_dump($string);
```

```
string(13) "Hello World!"
```

fwrite(*resource*, $string [,*length*])

Also known as **fputs()**
resource –Variable name containing the file pointer created by **fopen()**
length – [optional] **$integer** *default:* filesize(**$string**)

Writes the contents of **$string** to the file *resource* created by **fopen()**. If *length* is specified, writing will stop once *length* bytes or the end of **$string** has been reached.

Example:

```
$file = fopen('file.txt', 'a'); // appending on to the end
fwrite($file, 'Hello World!');
```

```
string(8) "Hello Wo"
```

See Also:

fwrite() – Writes to the opened file
fopen() – Opens a file for reading, writing, or both

To read the entire file into a string, use the function **filesize()**.

```
// file.txt contains the sentence: Hello World!
$filename = 'file.txt';
$file = fopen($filename, 'r');
$string = fread( $file, filesize($filename) );
var_dump($string);
```


```
// file.txt now contains at the end: Hello World!
```

filesize($string)

Returns an integer containing the length of the file with name/path of **$string**.
Note: *The results are cached. See* ***clearstatcache()****.*

Example:

```
// file.txt contains the word: Hello
var_dump( filesize('file.txt') );
```

```
int(5)
```

file($string [, *flags*])

flags – [optional] **$string** Values:

FILE_USE_INCLUDE_PATH (search for the file in include_path)
FILE_IGNORE_NEW_LINES (Don't add \n to end of array entries)
FILE_SKIP_EMPTY_LINES (skip empty lines)

Reads an entire file with filename **$string** line-by-line into an array, appending a newline (\n) to the end of each array entry (each entry is a line in the file), unless *flags* specifies otherwise.

Example:

```
// file.txt contains these tab delimited items:
// Bob  owner   34
// Mark manager 27
$array = file('file.txt');
echo '<pre>'; // Preformatted text, for readability
print_r($array);
```

```
Array
(
    [0] => Bob  owner   34
    [1] => Mark manager 27
)
```

See Also:

file_get_contents() – Similar, but returns a string instead of an array

file_get_contents($string [, *flags*] [, *context*] [, *start*] [, *max_length*])

flags – [optional] **$string** Values:

FILE_USE_INCLUDE_PATH (search for the file in include_path)

context – [optional] Ignore. Set to **NULL** if using *start* or *max_length*
start – [optional] **$integer** *default:* 0, beginning of the file
max_length – [optional] **$integer** *default:* filesize($string)
Reads an entire file with filename **$string** into a string. Starts at the beginning of the file unless *start* is specified, then it starts *start* position into

the file. If *max_length* is specified, only *max_length* bytes will be read into the string.

Examples:

```
// file.txt contains these tab delimited items:
// Bob  owner   34
// Mark manager 27
$string = file_get_contents('file.txt');
echo '<pre>'; // Preformatted text, for readability
var_dump($string);
```

```
string(29) "Bob owner   34
Mark    manager 27
"
```

```
$string = file_get_contents('file.txt', NULL, NULL, 5, 4);
echo '<pre>'; // Preformatted text, for readability
var_dump($string);
```

```
string(4) "wner"
```

See Also:

file() – Similar, but returns an array instead of a string

file_put_contents($string , *input* [, *flags*])

input – **$string** or **$array**
flags – [optional] **$string** Values:
FILE_USE_INCLUDE_PATH (search for the file in include_path)
FILE_APPEND (if file already exists, append instead of overwriting)
LOCK_EX (acquire an exclusive lock on the file for writing)
Equivalent to the combination of fopen(), fwrite(), and fclose().

Writes to the file with name/path of **$string** the contents of *input*. If *input* is an array, the entry values are combined as if they were one long string without a separating character. By default, if the file exists, it will be overwritten unless otherwise specified with *flags*.
Returns the number of bytes written to the file.

Examples:

```
$input = 'Hello World!';
file_put_contents('file.txt', $input);
```

```
// file.txt now contains: Hello World!
```

```
$input = array('Hello', 'World!');
file_put_contents('file.txt', $input);
```

```
// file.txt now contains: HelloWorld!
```

See Also:

file() – Reads a file into an array
file_get_contents() – Reads a file into a string

fprintf(*resource, formatting* [, *inputs* [, *...inputs...*]])

Accepts multiple inputs to be used when specified in formatting
resource –Variable name containing the file pointer created by **fopen()**
formatting – **$string**, see **sprintf()** for formatting guidelines
inputs – [optional] **$scalar**(s) to be formatted

Use *formating* to write to *resource* a string, using formatting rules (see **sprintf()**) and if supplied, the *inputs*. Returns the length of the outputted string.

Example:

```
$string = 'dog';
$file = fopen('file.txt', 'w');
$length = fprintf($file, "I like %ss.", $string);
```

```
// file.txt contains: I like dogs.
```

```
var_dump($length);
```

```
int(12)
```

See Also:

sprintf() – Formatting rules applied to strings
fwrite() – Writing to files with a specified string

fscanf(*resource, formatting* [, *outputs* [, *...inputs...*]])

Accepts multiple inputs to be used when specified in formatting
resource –Variable name containing the file pointer created by **fopen()**
formatting – **$string**, see **sprintf()** for formatting guidelines
outputs – [optional] Variable names to assign values to

Use *formating* to read from *resource* using formatting rules (see **sprintf()**) and if supplied, assigns the values to the *outputs*. Returns the values parsed by *formatting* as an array if no *inputs* were specified, otherwise it returns the number of assigned values.

Example:

```
// file.txt contains these tab delimited items:
// Bob  owner  34
// Mark manager 27
$file = fopen('file.txt', 'r');
$array = fscanf($file, "%s\t%s\t%s");
print_r($array);
```

```
Array
(
    [0] => Bob
    [1] => owner
    [2] => 34
)
```

```
$count = fscanf($file, "%s\t%s\t%s", $name, $title, $age);
echo "$name ($title) - $age";
```

```
Mark (manager) - 27
```

See Also:

sprintf() – Formatting rules applied to strings
sscanf() – Parses a string through a formatted string, reverse of **sprintf()**

fileatime($string)

Returns the time the file/path **$string** was last accessed, or FALSE upon failure. Returned value is a Unix timestamp.
Note: *The results are cached. See* ***clearstatcache()****.*

Example:

```
$timestamp = fileatime('tmp/file.txt');
echo date('m-d-Y g:i:sa', $timestamp);
```

```
03-20-2008 4:28:38am
```

See Also:

filemtime() – Similiar, but returns the last time the file was written

filemtime($string)

Returns the time the file/path **$string** was last written, or FALSE upon failure. Returned value is a Unix timestamp.
Note: *The results are cached. See* ***clearstatcache()****.*

Example:

```
$timestamp = filemtime('/opt/lampp/htdocs/file.txt');
echo date('m-d-Y g:i:sa', $timestamp);
```

```
03-20-2008 4:28:35am
```

See Also:

fileatime() – Similar, but returns the last time the file was accessed

file_exists($string)

Checks whether a file or directory with name/path of **$string** exists, returning TRUE if it does exist.
Note: *The results are cached. See* ***clearstatcache()****.*

Example:

```
// file.txt does exist
var_dump( file_exists('file.txt') );
```

```
bool(true)
```

is_readable($string)

Checks whether a file or directory with name/path of **$string** can be read, returning TRUE if it can be read.
Note: *The results are cached. See* ***clearstatcache()****.*

Example:

```
// file.txt is readable
var_dump( is_readable('file.txt') );
```

```
bool(true)
```

See Also:

file_exists() – Check whether a file exists

is_writable($string)

Commonly misspelled as is_writeable(), which is an alias
Checks whether a file or directory with name/path of **$string** can be written to, returning TRUE if it can be written to.
Note: *The results are cached. See* ***clearstatcache()****.*

Example:

```
// file.txt is writable
var_dump( is_writeable('file.txt') );
```

```
bool(true)
```

See Also:

file_exists() – Check whether a file exists

is_dir($string)

Checks whether **$string** is a directory, returning TRUE if it exists and is a directory.
Note: *The results are cached. See* ***clearstatcache()****.*

Examples:

```
// file.txt is a file, not a directory
var_dump( is_dir('file.txt') );
```

```
bool(false)
```

```
var_dump( is_dir('/opt/lampp/htdocs') );
```

```
bool(true)
```

See Also:

file_exists() – Check whether a file or directory exists
is_file() – Check whether a file exists and is actually a file

is_file($string)

Checks whether **$string** is a file, returning TRUE if it exists and is a file.
Note: *The results are cached. See **clearstatcache()**.*

Examples:

```
// file.txt exists
var_dump( is_file('file.txt') );
```

```
bool(true)
```

```
var_dump( is_file('/opt/lampp/htdocs') );
```

```
bool(false)
```

See Also:

file_exists() – Check whether a file or directory exists
is_dir() – Check whether a given path exists and is actually a directory

clearstatcache()

Clears the system cache of certain information gathered about files by specific functions, listed below. Used when a file is being altered and then reevaluated within the same script/page.
Effects the following functions: **file_exists()**, **is_writable()**, **is_readable()**, **is_file()**, **is_dir()**, **fileatime()**, **filemtime()**, **filesize()**, stat(), lstat(), is_executable(), is_link(), filectime(), fileinode(), filegroup(), fileowner(), filetype(), and fileperms().
Note: *If a file does not exist, PHP does not cache anything. See examples.*

Examples:

```
// file.txt does not yet exist, nothing will be cached
var_dump( file_exists('file.txt') );
file_put_contents('file.txt', 'Hello World!'); // create/write to file
var_dump( file_exists('file.txt') );
```

```
bool(false)
bool(true)
```

```
var_dump( file_exists('file.txt') );
// Some other script deletes the file in between here
var_dump( file_exists('file.txt') );
clearstatcache();
var_dump( file_exists('file.txt') );
```

```
bool(true)
bool(true)
bool(false)
```

chmod($string, *mode*)

mode – **$integer** (octal, leading zero)

Change the mode (permissions) for **$string** using the defined octal *mode*. ***Note:*** *Does not apply in Windows.*

Example:

```
chmod('file.txt', 0777);
```

```
// file.txt is now read/write/execute for everyone
```

Common octal modes:

```
0777 // Read, write, execute for everyone
0755 // Read/write/execute for owner, read/execute for others
0644 // Read/write for owner, read for everyone else
0600 // Read/write for owner, no access for anyone else
0754 // Read/write/execute for owner, read/execute group, read others
```

Output Control (Output Buffer)

Imagine all of your code, your output, stuffed into a big bag then dumped all at once on the counter, or if you prefer, thrown in the trash instead. The code still ran, just the output changed. That is output buffering in a nutshell. Furthermore, it also makes things easier, especially when dealing with headers and cookies, all requiring a specific order of output to the user.

flush()

Tries to push all output to the user/browser immediately rather than waiting till the script has completed.

Note: *If you are within an output buffer ob_start(), you need to also call* ***ob_flush().***

Examples:

```
for($x=0;$x<=1000;$x++){ // Loop through 1001 times
    echo $x;
    flush(); // Sends each echo $x to the browser
    // If flush() was not present, it would output the entire chain
    // of numbers to the browser at once when the script/loop was done
}
```

```
// Very long string of numbers: 12345678910111213... and so on
```

```
ob_start(); // Start an output buffer
for($x=0;$x<=1000;$x++){ // Loop through 1001 times
    echo $x;
    flush(); // Sends the output to the output buffer
    ob_flush(); // Sends the output buffer to the browser and clears it
    // If ob_flush() was not present, it would output the entire chain
    // of numbers to the browser at once when the script/loop was done
}
```

```
// Very long string of numbers: 12345678910111213... and so on
```

See Also:

ob_flush() – Flushes the output from the output buffer

♣ ♣ ♣

The use of **flush()** is used to give some feedback to the user running the script if it takes a while to run, otherwise they may be left with a blank page. For instance, when importing a lot of data to the database line-by-line from a file, you could provide a period (.) to the screen when each line is complete, and a line break every 70 periods or so, giving the user feedback that it is working. While this may be slower, it would be worse if they stopped the script thinking something was wrong.

As a comparison, a simple script is shown here and the varying time trials for each method used as a comparison.

```
/*
All of the below methods use the following code around it to generate
the time to complete. The output shown is only the time to complete,
not the long string of numbers that would be echoed as well.
*/
$time = microtime(1); // At the start
// Examples go here
$time = number_format(microtime(1)-$time, 6);
echo "$time seconds to complete"; // At the end
```

Examples:

```
for($x=0;$x<=100000;$x++){
    echo $x;
}
```

```
0.468251 seconds to complete
```

```
for($x=0;$x<=100000;$x++){
    echo $x;
    flush();
}
```

```
3.616512 seconds to complete
```

```
ob_start();
for($x=0;$x<=100000;$x++){
    echo $x;
}
```

```
0.182167 seconds to complete
```

```
ob_start();
for($x=0;$x<=100000;$x++){
    echo $x;
    flush();
  // Won't output to the user until script completes w/o ob_flush()
}
```

```
0.762600 seconds to complete
```

```
ob_start();
for($x=0;$x<=100000;$x++){
    echo $x;
    flush();
    ob_flush();
}
```

```
4.443787 seconds to complete
```

readfile($string [, *use_include_path*])

use_include_path – [optional] **$boolean** *default:* FALSE

Reads the contents of the file with name/path **$string** and writes it to the output, similar to reading the contents into a string and then **echo**ing the string. If *use_include_path* is set to TRUE, the file is searched for within the PHP include_path.

Example:

```
// file.txt contains: Hello World
readfile('file.txt');
```

```
Hello World
```

ob_start([*callback_function*] [, *flush_size*] [, *erase*])

callback_function – [optional] **$string** (function name)
flush_size – [optional] **$integer** *default:* 0 (flush at the end)
Other preset values: 1 (set the size to 4096)
erase – [optional] **$boolean** *default:* TRUE, buffer cleared at *flush_size*

Starts an output buffer, storing all output before sending it to the user/browser at once at the end of the script, or when specified by other ob_*() functions. The end of the script closes the buffer.
If a *callback_function* is specified, the output stored in the buffer is sent as a string to the function with the name *callback_function* when the script is completed or **ob_end_flush()** is called. The function should return a string so it can be output to the user/browser.
If *flush_size* is set, the buffer will be flushed (same as **ob_flush()**) when a section of output causes the buffer to exceed the *flush_size* length. If *erase* is set to FALSE, the buffer is not deleted until the script finishes.
Note: *Returns FALSE if the function specified in callback_function fails.*

Examples:

```
ob_start();
// Some code generating output here
```

```
// Output is sent at the end of the script
```

```
function ChangeName($buffer){
    // Replace all instances of 'username' with 'Bob' in the buffer
    $buffer = str_replace('username', 'Bob', $buffer);
    return $buffer; // Return for output the new buffer
}
ob_start('ChangeName');
echo 'My name is username';
```

```
My name is Bob
```

```
function ChangeName($buffer){
    $buffer = $buffer . '||'; // Add || to the end of the buffer
    return $buffer;
}
ob_start('ChangeName',10);
echo 'My name is Mario';
echo 'My name is Mario';
```

```
My name is Mario||My name is Mario||
```

There is a predefined function called ob_gzhandler that will compress the buffer prior to sending the output to the user/browser. To call it, use:

```
ob_start('ob_gzhandler');
```

The output buffer reorganizes the output of **header()** and **setcookie()** automatically to the top of the page so there are no Apache errors. This makes it easy to include a redirect in **header()** somewhere in your script if something fails, even if you have output data already to the page earlier in the script. The redirect and header information is placed first and the user never sees the data.

```
ob_start();
echo 'You will never see this';
if ($baduser){ // If $baduser is TRUE
    header('Location: http://www.someotherplace.com');
}
ob_end_flush; // Ends the buffer and sends the output to the user
```

ob_flush()

Sends all the contents of the buffer to the user/browser as if you had reached the end of the script, erasing the current contents of the buffer. The buffer is not closed.

Example:

```
ob_start();
echo 'Send me now!';
ob_flush();
echo 'Send me at the end of the script.';
```

```
Send me now!Send me at the end of the script.
```

ob_clean()

Discard/delete the current contents of the output buffer. The buffer is not closed.

Example:

```
ob_start();
echo 'I will never be seen';
ob_clean();
echo 'Send me at the end of the script.';
```

```
Send me at the end of the script.
```

ob_end_flush()

Sends all the contents of the current output buffer to the user/browser as if you had reached the end of the script, erasing the current contents of the buffer. The buffer is then closed. This function is called automatically at the end of the script/page that has **ob_start()** present.

Example:

```
ob_start();
echo 'Send me now!';
ob_end_flush();
// The rest of the code is not buffered.
```

```
Send me now!
```

ob_end_clean()

Discard/delete the current contents of the current output buffer, then close the buffer.

Example:

```
ob_start();
echo 'I will never be seen';
ob_end_clean();
// The following code is not buffered
echo 'Send me at the end of the script.';
```

```
Send me at the end of the script.
```

ob_get_flush()

Returns a string with all the contents of the current output buffer, flushes/sends the contents of the buffer to the user/browser, erases the current contents of the buffer and finally closes it.

Example:

```
ob_start();
echo 'Send me, store me. ';
$buffer = ob_get_flush(); // Buffer is now closed
echo "buffer: $buffer";
```

```
Send me, store me. buffer: Send me, store me.
```

ob_get_clean()

Return the contents of the current buffer to a string then discard/delete the current contents of the buffer, finally closing the buffer.

Example:

```
ob_start();
echo 'I will exist in a string';
$buffer = ob_get_clean(); // Buffer is now closed
echo "buffer: $buffer";
```

```
buffer: I will exist in a string
```

ob_get_contents()

Returns a string with all the contents of the current output buffer without clearing it. The buffer is <u>not</u> closed.

Example:

```
ob_start();
echo 'Send me, store me. ';
$buffer = ob_get_contents();
ob_end_clean(); // Close and erase the buffer
echo "buffer: $buffer";
```

```
buffer: Send me, store me.
```

ob_get_length()

Returns an integer with the length of the current output buffer.

Example:

```
ob_start();
echo 'Hello World!';
var_dump( ob_get_length() );
echo 'Hello again...';
var_dump( ob_get_length() );
```

```
Hello World!int(12)
Hello again...int(34)
```

ob_get_level()

Returns an integer containing the number of output buffers deep it is nested within, or 0 if output buffering is not enabled.

Example:

```
var_dump( ob_get_level() );
ob_start(); // First output buffer
ob_start(); // Second output buffer
var_dump( ob_get_level() );
```

```
int(0) int(2)
```

Sessions

Sessions are used in PHP to provide a method to track a user throughout a website and pass data between pages about that user during their time on the site. A unique ID is assigned to the user and the data is stored on the server itself, rather than on the user's computer such as with cookies. The most common form of session usage is for commerce sites and the ability to have a shopping cart, user login and customized interfaces, and navigation history.

session_start()

Start a new session or continue an already open session based on the current session id stored in a cookie or passed through GET or POST.
***Note:** If using the **ob_start()** function, place it before **session_start()**. Secondarily, **session_start()** must be called prior to any other output is generated when **ob_start()** is not used.*

Examples:

```
session_start();
echo "Your session id is " . session_id();
```

```
Your session id is 11b049bff9515e18bc1fe04c75ee9d7b
```

```
session_start();
$_SESSION['color'] = 'blue';
```

```
The value 'blue' is assigned to the session with the key 'color'
```

session_unset()

Unset/remove all session variables, essentially removing all entries in the $_SESSION global variable array.
***Note:** If you want to unset a specific key, use unset($_SESSION['key']).*

Example:

```
session_start();
$_SESSION['color'] = 'blue';
echo $_SESSION['color'];
session_unset();
echo $_SESSION['color'];
```

```
blue
Notice: Undefined index: color in /opt/lampp/htdocs/test.php on line 27
```

See Also:

session_destroy() – Destroy everything related to a session

session_destroy()

Destroy/delete the current session. The values stored in $_SESSION are not deleted[22] and any session cookies are also not deleted (see tip below). ***Note:*** *It is necessary to call* ***session_start()*** *again after* ***session_destroy()*** *if you still want to have a session.*

Example:

```
session_start();
$_SESSION['color'] = 'blue';
echo $_SESSION['color'];
session_unset();
echo $_SESSION['color'];
```

```
blue
Notice: Undefined index: color in /opt/lampp/htdocs/test.php on line 27
```

See Also:

session_unset() – Remove all variables assigned to $_SESSION
session_regenerate_id() – Recreate a new session id
setcookie() – Create or delete a cookie

To completely destroy the session, you must destroy the cookie as well. This is done using the **setcookie()** function.

```
session_start(); // Load session
session_destroy(); // Destroy session
session_unset(); // Delete all variables in $_SESSION
setcookie( session_name(), '', time()-1 );
```

```
// Sets the cookie to expire 1 second ago, essentially deleting it
```

22 Use **session_unset()** or **$_SESSION = array();** to remove session variables

session_name([$string])

Returns the name of the session. If **$string** is provided, the session name is set to the value of **$string**. The default session name if session_name() is not used is PHPSESSID.

Note: *If setting the session name, it should be called prior to* ***session_start()****.*

Example:

```
session_name('SessionName');
session_start();
echo session_name();
```

```
SessionName
```

session_id([$string]))

Return a string containing the session id. If **$string** is provided, the session id is set to the value of **$string**.

Note: *If setting the session id, it should be called prior to* ***session_start()****.*

Example:

```
session_id('1234567890abcdefgh');
session_start();
echo session_id();
```

```
1234567890abcdefgh
```

session_regenerate_id([*delete_old_session*]))

delete_old_session – [optional] **$boolean** *default:* FALSE, keep the same session

Generates a new session id, without losing any of the current session information other than the id. If *delete_old_session* is set to TRUE, the old associated session file is deleted.

Example:

```
session_start();
echo session_id() . ' || ';
session_regenerate_id();
echo session_id();
```

```
3469a2bb3764ab6c4eccd9582140637f || 3e4a35dbe6def6a179d7625bf88beb32
```

session_write_close()

Ends the current session and stores the current session data. This occurs automatically at the end of the script/page, but may be used to allow faster access to the session information since it is locked to one script at a time.

Example:

```
session_start();
session_write_close(); // Would be done at the end of the page anyway
```

Regular Expressions

Sometimes you want to check for a specific structure as opposed to a specific value. Regular expressions allow this type of matching. Besides the few examples below and the inclusion of some regular expression syntax, no tutorial on regular expressions is given here (that could be its own book).

Regular Expression Syntax

^ – Start of string
$ – End of string
. – Any single character
( ) – Group of expressions
[] – Item range (*e.g.* [afg] means a, f, or g)
[^] – Items not in range (*e.g.* [^cde] means not c, d, or e)
- (dash) – character range within an item range (*e.g.* [a-z] means a through z)
| (pipe) – Logical or (*e.g.* (a|b) means a or b)
? – Zero or one of preceding character/item range
* – Zero or more of preceding character/item range
+ – One or more of preceding character/item range
{*integer*} – Exactly *integer* of preceding character/item range (*e.g.* a{2})
{*integer,*} – *Integer* or more of preceding character/item range (*e.g.* a{2,})
{*integer,integer*} – From *integer* to *integer* (*e.g.* a{2,4} means 2 to four of a)
\ – Escape character
[:punct:] – Any punctuation
[:space:] – Any space character
[:blank:] – Any space or tab
[:digit:] – Any digit: 0 through 9
[:alpha:] – All letters: a-z and A-Z
[:alnum:] – All digits and letters: 0-9, a-z, and A-Z
[:xdigit:] – Hexadecimal digit
[:print:] – Any printable character
[:upper:] – All uppercase letters: A-Z
[:lower:] – All lowercase letters: a-z

<u>**PERL Compatible (PCRE) only**</u> (preg_*())
/ - delimiter before and after the expression

Character classes:
\c – Control character
\s – Whitespace
\S – Not whitespace
\d – Digit (0-9)
\D – Not a digit
\w – Letter (a-z, A-Z)
\W – Not a letter
\x – Hexadecimal digit
\O – Octal digit

Modifiers:
i – Case-insensitive
s – Period matches newline
m – ^ and $ match lines
U – Ungreedy matching
e – Evaluate replacement
x – Pattern over several lines

ereg(*pattern*, $string [, *group_array*])

pattern – **$string** Regular expression
group_array – [optional] Name of array to use for regular expression groups

Matches the regular expression in *pattern* against **$string**. If items in *pattern* are grouped (), supplying the variable name for an array to assign those group's values to is set as *group_array*[23].
Returns FALSE on failed match, 1 if *group_array* is not provided, and the length of **$string** if *group_array* is provided.

Examples:

```
$regex = "^[A-Z][a-z]+$";
// start, one uppercase letter, one or more lowercase letters, end
$string = "Hello";
var_dump( ereg($regex, $string) );
```

```
int(1)
```

```
$regex = "^([A-Z][a-z]+)[[:space:]]+([[:alpha:]]+)$";
// start, (one uppercase letter, one or more lowercase letters)
// one or more spaces, (one or more letters), end
$string = "Hello World";
```

23 The array in *group_array* will contain the entire string as key [0]

```
var_dump( ereg($regex, $string, $array) );
print_r($array);
```

```
int(11)
Array
(
    [0] => Hello World
    [1] => Hello
    [2] => World
)
```

See Also:

eregi() – Case-insensitive version of **ereg()**

eregi(*pattern*, $string [, *group_array*])

pattern – **$string** Regular expression
group_array – [optional] Name of array to use for regular expression groups

Matches the regular expression in *pattern* against **$string** in a case-insensitive manner. If items in *pattern* are grouped (), supplying the variable name for an array to assign those group's values to is set as *group_array*[24].
Returns FALSE on failed match, 1 if *group_array* is not provided, and the length of **$string** if *group_array* is provided.

Example:

```
$regex = "^[a-z]+$";
$string = "Hello";
var_dump( eregi($regex, $string) );
```

```
int(1)
```

See Also:

ereg() – Case-sensitive version of **eregi()**

ereg_replace(*pattern*, *replacement*, $string)

pattern – **$string** Regular expression
replacement – **$string** *digit* represents group () matches

Returns a string containing **$string** after being evaluated by *pattern* regular expression and replacing it with the format in *replacement*.

Items placed in groups (parenthesis) within the regular expression *pattern* can be reused within *replacement* and referred to by *digit*, with \\0 representing all of **$string** and \\1 equal to the first grouped match, \\2 the second, etc.
Note: *If no matches are found, the original **$string** is returned.*

24 The array in *group_array* will contain the entire string as key [0]

Examples:

```
$string = 'Hello';
$pattern = "^([A-Z])[a-z]+$";
// pattern: start, 1 uppercase letter, one or more lowercase, end
$replacement = ".\\1.\\0.";
// replacement: put periods around first group and whole string
$newstring = ereg_replace($pattern, $replacement, $string);
echo $newstring;
```

```
.H.Hello.
```

```
$string = '5551234567'; // phone number without punctuation
$pattern = "^([0-9]{3})([[:digit:]]{3})([0-9]{4})$";
$replacement = "(\\1)\\2-\\3";
// replacement: put formatting around a phone number
$newstring = ereg_replace($pattern, $replacement, $string);
echo $newstring;
```

```
(555)123-4567
```

See Also:

str_replace() – Find and replace exact matches within a string
eregi_replace() – Case-insensitive version of **ereg_replace()**

eregi_replace(*pattern, replacement,* $string)

pattern – **$string** Regular expression
replacement – **$string** *digit* represents group () matches (*e.g.* \\0 whole string)

Returns a string containing **$string** after being evaluated by *pattern* regular expression and replacing it with the format in *replacement*. Items placed in groups (parenthesis) within the regular expression *pattern* can be reused within *replacement* and referred to by *digit,* with \\0 representing all of **$string** and \\1 equal to the first grouped match, \\2 the second, etc.
Note: *If no matches are found, the original* ***$string*** *is returned.*

Example:

```
$string = 'Hello';
$pattern = "^([a-z])[a-z]+$";
// pattern: start, one letter, one or more letters, end
$replacement = ".\\1.\\0.";
// replacement: put periods around first group and whole string
$newstring = eregi_replace($pattern, $replacement, $string);
echo $newstring;
```

```
.H.Hello.
```

See Also:

str_ireplace() – Replace exact matches within a string, case-insensitive
ereg_replace() – Case-sensitive version of **eregi_replace()**

split(*pattern*, $string [, *limit*])

pattern – **$string** Regular expression
limit – [optional] **$integer** *default:* -1, no limit

Returns an array that is created by splitting the contents of **$string** based upon the provided regular expression *pattern*. If *limit* is specified, it sets the maximum number of entries in the array, with the last one being the remaining portion of **$string** that was not processed.
Note: *If limit is set to 1, the array will contain only **$string**.*

Examples:

```
$string = '2-01-2008';
$pattern = '[[:punct:]]'; // Any single punctuation character
$array = split($pattern, $string);
print_r($array);
```

```
Array
(
    [0] => 2
    [1] => 01
    [2] => 2008
)
```

```
$string = '2-01-2008';
$pattern = '[[:punct:]]'; // Any single punctuation character
$array = split($pattern, $string, 2);
print_r($array);
```

```
Array
(
    [0] => 2
    [1] => 01-2008
)
```

See Also:

spliti() – Case-insensitive version of **split()**
explode() – Spits a string into an array based upon an exact match string

spliti(*pattern*, $string [, *limit*])

pattern – **$string** Regular expression
limit – [optional] **$integer** *default:* -1, no limit

Returns an array that is created by splitting the contents of **$string** based upon the provided regular expression *pattern* in a case-insensitive manner.

If *limit* is specified, it sets the maximum number of entries in the array, with the last one being the remaining portion of **$string** that was not processed.
Note: *If limit is set to 1, the array will contain only **$string**.*

Example:

```
$string = 'abcdef abCdef abcdef';
$pattern = '[c]';
$array = spliti($pattern, $string);
print_r($array);
```

```
Array
(
    [0] => ab
    [1] => def ab
    [2] => def ab
    [3] => def
)
```

See Also:

split() – Case-sensitive version of **spliti()**
explode() – Spits a string into an array based upon an exact match string

preg_replace(*pattern, replacement, subject* [*, limit*] [*, count*])

pattern – **$string** or **$array** Regular expression(s)
replacement – **$string** or **$array**
subject – **$string** or **$array**
limit – [optional] **$integer** *default:* -1, no limit
count – [optional] Variable name to contain an **$integer**

Replaces all instances matching *pattern* with *replacement* within *subject*. If *subject* is an array, the match and replace occurs on all entries within the array.
To refer to groups () created in *pattern* within the *replacement*, use \${*digit*}, where \${0} represents the entire string, \${1} is the first group, and so on.
If *pattern* and *replacement* are arrays, the entire *subject* is processed for each entry in the arrays, finding the first entry in *pattern* and replacing it with the first entry in *replacement*, then repeating with the next set of entries. If there are more values in the *pattern* array than the *replacement* array, an empty string ('') is used as the replacement. If *pattern* is an array and *replacement* is a string, it is used for every entry in *pattern*.
The optional *count* variable will be set with the total number of replacements that occurred.
***Note:** This is PERL/PCRE, and the expression delimiter (/) may be used with the modifiers at the end of the expression.*

Example:

```
$pattern = "/^(\d{3})(\d{3})(\d{4})$/";
$replacement = "(\${1})\${2}-\${3}";
$subject = '5551234567';
$result = preg_replace($pattern, $replacement, $subject, -1, $count);
echo "result: $result, count: $count";
```

```
result: (555)123-4567, count: 1
```

See Also:

Regular Expression Syntax – Includes PERL/PCRE specific items
str_replace() – Find and replace exact match strings within a string

preg_split(*pattern*, $string [, *limit*] [, *flags*])

pattern – **$string** Regular expression
limit – [optional] **$integer** *default:* -1, no limit
flags – [optional] **$string** *default:* none
Values: PREG_SPLIT_NOEMPTY (return only non-empty pieces)
PREG_SPLIT_DELIM_CAPTURE (parenthesized delimiters inside of *pattern* will be returned in the array as well)
PREG_SPLIT_OFFSET_CAPTURE (for each match, an entry is made to include its position (characters from start)

Returns an array containing the contents of **$string** after being split based upon the regular expression *pattern*. If *limit* is specified, it sets the maximum number of entries in the array, with the last one being the remaining portion of **$string** that was not processed. The optional *flags* provide extra functionality described above.
Note: *If limit is set to 1, the array will contain only **$string**.*
Note: *This is PERL/PCRE, and the expression delimiter (/) may be used with the modifiers at the end of the expression.*

Examples:

```
$string = '2-01-2008';
$pattern = '/\D/'; // Split on anything that is not a digit
$array = preg_split($pattern, $string);
print_r($array);
```

```
Array
(
    [0] => 2
    [1] => 01
    [2] => 2008
)
```

```
$string = '2-01-2008';
$pattern = '/(\D)/'; // Split on anything that is not a digit
$array = preg_split($pattern, $string, -1, PREG_SPLIT_DELIM_CAPTURE);
print_r($array);
```

```
Array
(
    [0] => 2
    [1] => -
    [2] => 01
    [3] => -
    [4] => 2008
)
```

```
$string = '2-01-2008';
$pattern = '/\D/'; // Split on anything that is not a digit
$array = preg_split($pattern, $string, 2, PREG_SPLIT_OFFSET_CAPTURE);
print_r($array);
```

```
Array
(
    [0] => Array
        (
            [0] => 2
            [1] => 0
        )
    [1] => Array
        (
            [0] => 01-2008
            [1] => 2
        )
)
```

preg_match(*pattern*, $string [, *group_array*] [, *flag*] [, *offset*])

pattern – **$string** Regular expression
group_array – [optional] Name of array to use for regular expression groups
flag – [optional] **$string** *default:* none
Value: PREG_OFFSET_CAPTURE for each match, an entry is made to include its position (characters from start)
offset – [optional] *default:* 0, start of the string

Checks **$string** for a regular expression match in *pattern*. If items in *pattern* are grouped (), supplying the variable name for an array to assign those group's values to and is set as *group_array*[25]. The optional *offset* can specify how many characters from the beginning of **$string** to start from, though it can have conflicts with regular expression syntax such as ^ and $ in *pattern*. Returns the number of matches: 1 if matched, 0 if no match, and FALSE on error.

25 The array in *group_array* will contain the entire string as key [0]

Examples:

```
$pattern = "/^(\w+)\s(\w+)$/i"; // Using case-insensitive modifier: i
// Pattern: start, one or more letters, space, one or more letters, end
$string = 'Hello world';
var_dump( preg_match($pattern, $string) );
```

```
int(1)
```

```
$pattern = "/(\w+)\s(\w+)/i"; // Using case-insensitive modifier: i
// Pattern: one or more letters, single space, one or more letters
$string = 'Hello world';
var_dump( preg_match($pattern, $string, $array) );
print_r($array);
```

```
int(1)
Array
(
    [0] => Hello world
    [1] => Hello
    [2] => world
)
```

See Also:

preg_match_all() – Checks for multiple matches within a string

preg_match_all(*pattern*, $string, *group_array* [, *flag*] [, *offset*])

pattern – **$string** Regular expression
group_array – Variable name of array to use for regular expression groups
flag – [optional] **$string** *default:* none
Values: PREG_PATTERN_ORDER (Order results so that *group_array*[0] contains full pattern matches, *group_array*[1] contains first group, etc.)
PREG_SET_ORDER (Order *group_array* by set of matches)
PREG_OFFSET_CAPTURE for each match, an entry is made to include its position (characters from start)
offset – [optional] *default:* 0, start of the string

Checks **$string** for a regular expression match in *pattern*. If items in *pattern* are grouped (), *group_array* represents an array to assign those group's values to and is set as *group_array*. The optional *offset* can specify how many characters from the beginning of **$string** to start from, though it can have conflicts with regular expression syntax such as ^ and $ in *pattern*.
Returns the number of matches or FALSE on an error.

Example:

```
$pattern = "/(\w+)/i"; // Using case-insensitive modifier: i
// Pattern: start, one or more letters, space, one or more letters, end
$string = 'Hello world';
var_dump( preg_match_all($pattern, $string, $array) );
print_r($array);
```

```
int(2)
Array
(
    [0] => Array
        (
            [0] => Hello
            [1] => world
        )
    [1] => Array
        (
            [0] => Hello
            [1] => world
        )
)
```

See Also:

preg_match() – Checks for a single regular expression match within a string

Common Language Index

Function Index

Printed in Great Britain
by Amazon.co.uk, Ltd.,
Marston Gate.